waiting

for

MY

cats

to die

ALSO BY STACY HORN

Cyberville: Clicks, Culture and the
Creation of an Online Town

A MEMOIR

STACY HORN

waiting

for

my

cats

to die

St. Martin's Griffin ❧ New York

www.stmartins.com

Design by Kathryn Parise

"Beyond the Blue Horizon," written by Leo Robin, Richard A. Whiting, and W. Franke Harling. Copyright © 1930 by Famous Music Corporation. Copyright renewed 1957 by Famous Music Corporation.

Lyrics from "After the Ball" written by Charles K. Harris.

Lyrics from "Poor Wand'ring One" written by W. S. Gilbert and Sir Arthur Sullivan.

Lyrics from the song that begins "Arouse my brother Minute Men" (song has no official title) written by S. Mills.

Library of Congress Cataloging-in-Publication Data

Horn, Stacy.
    Waiting for my cats to die : a memoir / Stacy Horn.
        p. cm.
    ISBN 0-312-26692-8 (hc)
    ISBN 0-312-28744-5 (pbk)
    Midlife crisis—Miscellanea. I. Title.

BF724.65.M53 H67 2001
305.24'4'092—dc21   00-047040
[B]

First St. Martin's Griffin Edition: January 2002

10 9 8 7 6 5 4 3 2 1

to my oldest friend, christine Hegarty,
and to all my friends in the secret space

introduction

THIS IS HOW I LIVE: the same way I watch TV, hitting that channel button every few seconds, relentlessly scanning. I use my television set like a slide projector. The light in my living room flashes on and off—next, next, next. There are so few shows worth looking at too closely, or for more than a few minutes at a time. My life? No different. I don't stay on any one thing for too long. So if you get bored, you won't be bored for long.

My problems. First, I watch far too much TV. To give you an idea, this is me on Echo, the online service I founded and which is in trouble, where people log on to talk about whatever: "Why didn't someone tell me it was this late? Here I've been, reading and writing for God knows how many hours, when I could have been watching *West Wing*. Do me a favor? If you

1

ever see me logged in during the important TV hours, please remind me to log off."

Second, I'm forty-two and single, and while I have pronounced myself ready to settle down, I am as far from marriage or anything like it as I was when I was sixteen. I'm lonely and yet don't make a tenth of the effort with romance that I make in every other area of my life. I work at least eight hours a day. Why don't I spend even half that looking for love? I'm a coward. No, it's because I want it this way. My friend Steven says I could be married within a year if I really wanted to be. No! It's because there are no men. It's not my fault. That's it. No, I scare them. A popular explanation with other single women I know. There's something flattering and also comforting about thinking we're intimidating. If we weren't so fabulous and strong, everything would be okay. Right. Crazy people find true love. People in prison manage to get married. There must be something wrong with me. "There's something terribly wrong with me and no one will tell me what it is," I insist to my friends. I don't know. I don't know how I got here.

Third, as I said, Echo, my business, is in trouble. I don't care, really. I am sick to death of new media. I would much, much rather watch TV. It's time to move on. But how am I going to pay for this laptop I'm typing on? My first book didn't sell well. No one wants my novel. I don't know what I'm going to do with myself. Not one single area of my life is settled. Oh, and I have two diabetic cats: Veets and Beamers. I have to give them insulin injections every twelve hours. It's worse than that. Beamers has failing kidneys and has to get a subcutaneous drip every other day, and he also has a stomach thing I can't spell or pronounce. When I meet new people and tell them about my cat situation, they ask, "Why don't you kill them?" People. Because I can lean down and sniff my cats' heads and smell earth and trees and leaves—it's a swampy smell, the scent of eternity, the opposite of the smell of bleakness. A small comfort perhaps, after all that work, but that pretty much describes everything.

Last, I spend way too much time with death. I buy every death book, go to every death movie. Instead of tripping from club to club like the party girl I was in my youth, I spend my free time going through boxes in abandoned basements and attics and hacking my way through vines and thorns in forgotten cemeteries. I want to unearth the unremembered, because if I can resurrect these abandoned histories, I win. That's what it feels like, anyway.

This is about my midlife crisis—or rather, my early-onset midlife crisis. I'm always rushing things. If something bad is going to happen I'd just as soon have it happen now and get it over with. I'm writing about what I'm going through while it happens because writing about it contains it and makes me feel like I'm one step ahead of the game. I'd read about midlife if I could, except there's nothing out there that doesn't feel like work to read. Gail Sheehy makes me want to hit someone. I admit I've never read her, but the idea of a book called *Passages* annoys me. I think life basically sucks. I'm stealing from my friend Liz Margoshes, who says, "Life sucks, essentially." (I have to give credit where credit is due.) Growing old is not so freaking wonderful. What is wrong with people? I hate Lauren Bacall and that supposedly healthy I've-earned-my-wrinkles, dammit attitude that she and others have. Lauren, what follows growing old? Death, thank you. If Gail Sheehy had named her book *Passages Suck but What Are You Going to Do?* she would have had me.

I went to a conference called Hope a couple of months ago and the most hopeful thing I heard was this: "Life is hard, with a couple of moments of glory in between." I don't remember who said it, so I cannot give credit where credit is due. I only bring it up to head the well-why-don't-you-just-kill-yourself people off at the pass. (I don't know what "off at the pass" means, exactly.) A few moments of glory. It's enough.

We've all read about how men act out their midlife crises over and over and over. Yeah, yeah. What do women do? This book will show you. I've started to act out in all sorts of ways. My pain will be your amusement. I'll flip through the various channels of my life, going back to some more often than others because there's more happening on these channels, or because I'm more obsessed with these channels, or because I can't help making the same mistakes over and over—Don't sleep with musicians, *Don't sleep with musicians*—it's my new rule, which I will ignore the second I get an opportunity, except those opportunities don't come like they used to, like the every-weekend glory of my twenties. And guess what? It only gets worse.

I don't know what I'm going to do. I'd like to give it all up and hit the road, where it is easier to pretend that everything goes on forever. I'm just waiting for my cats to die. Then I'll quit. But is quitting liberation? Or hiding? Who am I kidding. It's an excuse. Like my life is my cats' fault and I'm off the hook until they're dead. My cats must live forever.

This is hard. Growing old is hard. Plus I'm alone. And then there are my sick cats. I'm scared. But not always.

MUSIC

I DIDN'T SEE IT COMING. One minute my future is endless, and the next minute I have a stomach and a very very short time left before I die, horribly—and I know I will. I read the peaceful-death-fantasy-shattering accounts in Sherwin B. Nuland's book *How We Die*. (It's going to be bad.) I finished it just before my fortieth birthday, which I then spent in sheer, mortal panic. *Now what are you going to do, now what are you going to do, oh God oh God oh God*, my thoughts ran, like a faucet turned on full blast. Then I thought, *Well, there's always the rock star option*, and everything was okay again. Like everyone else in the United States, and perhaps the entire Western world—not that I would know, I never go anywhere—I have fantasies about being a rock star. It would save me. It gives my panic a direction. *You're going to be a rock star now. Okay. It's going to be okay.* Except I don't have much of a voice, I can't play the guitar,

5

the essential rock star instrument, and I only took a year's worth of piano lessons. *I'm so unprepared*, I think. Where should I start?

Twenty years ago I was sitting on the corner in the West Village of Manhattan, where I live, where I've lived for my entire adult life, watching the Halloween parade, when a pack of drummers marched by. There had to have been over fifty of them. I stood up and started dancing in the street. I danced with them for twenty blocks straight. I didn't stop until they stopped. Now, I am not a dancing-in-the-streets kind of girl. I would like to think I am, instead of the overly self-conscious, trapped, and paralyzed person that I am, who chants, "I hate myself, I hate myself, I hate myself," every morning in the shower. Why couldn't I be more like my friend Aly's girlfriend, the pretty, vivacious, and Italian Maria? Of course, she *had* to be from Rome on top of everything else. I met Maria around the same time I first heard the drummers, when we were both just starting out in life. I was a small, dark troll beside the light and lovely and carefree Maria. Watching her made me ache. Maria would have danced in the streets and not thought twice about it. I *would* think about it. For the next twenty years I would think about it. But it wasn't the dancing I couldn't forget. It was the drumming.

Then, just before I turned forty, I read about a group of drummers called the Manhattan Samba Group. I was sure these were the same guys. I called them. Six months later I was drumming in the Halloween parade. I was so terrified about fucking up that I could have been in any city on any day, and not in front of thousands of oddly dressed people screaming and cheering us on block after block. All I could concentrate on was getting it right. *Must!* (drum-drum) *not!* (drum-drum) *make!* (drum-drum) *any!* (drum-drum) *mistakes!* I thought, head down, staring furiously. The angry little drummer girl. I don't think I looked up from my drum once.

The following summer I ran into Maria. I hadn't seen her for twenty years. *Quit haunting me, Maria.* I had met her at the beginning of my adult life; then she moved back to Rome, and now I've hit the middle and here she was again. Only now, everything about her was all wrong. There was something funny about her mouth. She carried herself like she was still vivacious, but it was as if someone had thrown a blanket over her head. She was muffled. What had been charming in a twenty-year-old was just a little bit unsettling in a forty-year-old who wasn't pulling it off anymore. I fled. I couldn't talk to her. When I was twenty I couldn't talk to her because all I could think about was what a loser I was. I couldn't talk to her when I was forty because she was still supposed to be the life of the party and she wasn't. There was something funny about her mouth. It was the first time I could remember staring mortality in the face, and okay, I'd rather feel like a loser.

So now I'm a regular member of the Manhattan Samba Group. We drum every Saturday night at SOB's (Sounds of Brazil) from two to four o-fucking-clock in the morning, which makes Sunday a total waste of a day for me. I don't care. I never really liked Sundays anyway. They're supposed to be peaceful, a day of rest. The only thing I've ever felt on Sundays is dread.

I'm not a rock star, but I'm close enough. Sometimes when we walk through the crowd, carrying our drums up to the stage, a few people raise their fists and yell "Manhattan Samba!"

cats

First I'll explain my cats' names. I might as well get that humiliation over with. The older of the two is Veets. That's short for VTAM (vee-tam), which stands for virtual telecommunications access method, an obsolete IBM computer thing that's not worth explaining. Yes, it's a stupid name and goes firmly into the "seemed like a good idea at the time" category, but the story has its sweet side. Veets was given to me fourteen years ago by Don, the man I was engaged to marry. Don got him from the Center for Animal Care and Control, the place where people leave pets they don't want to keep. If no one adopts them they're killed. Don taught me VTAM, which I needed for a job I was desperate to get. I got the job, so I named the cat VTAM; then I went into a deep depression. We ended up breaking the engagement, Don moved to California, and that is the origin of my unnaturally close relationship with Veets. We bonded over our mutual, sorry, alone-again-naturally state. A year later, after a period of the kind of drinking that makes every awful thing worse, I checked myself into a rehab and that leads to my second cat, Beams, or Beamer(s). Beams is from "Seymour." Seymour-Bemore-Beamers-Beams. I got Beamers a few weeks after I got out of the rehab. I named him for Seymour Glass from the J. D. Salinger books and stories. An odd choice. I was feeling so hopeful, and yet I named him for a character who commits suicide.

On the way back from the Center for Animal Care and Control, Beamers started trembling and throwing up in the little brown cardboard box they gave me to take him home. "He hasn't been weaned," the vet told me. For a week I had to hold him in one hand and feed him milk from an eyedropper with the other, and that is the origin of my unnaturally close relationship with Beamers. When he took his first bite of food, I threw his tiny, furry body up in the air in triumph, like a parent with a child who has taken his first step.

Now, here's what I really mean by unnaturally close. A couple of years ago a fire broke out in my building. I was frantic. I only had one cat carrier, where I put Beams, and nothing to hold Veets. I tried a pillowcase, a piece of carry-on luggage, and a purse. The room was filling with smoke, I was panicking, but I couldn't leave without Veets. I went out onto my fire escape to get some air and to think my situation through. I realized then that there was simply no way I was going to leave him there to die, and that that meant I was going to die, too. In a particularly painful way, just like Sherwin B. Nuland said I would. Me and Veets and Beams were going to die. I sat there contemplating that for a minute or two. We're all going to die. I tried to leave. I tried to leave by walking down the fire escape, but by the second step I was in tears. I sat down again. *I'm really going to die.* Fortunately, we were saved by a fireman who called up to tell me that the fire was out and that I didn't have to leave the building after all.

This is what the cats I would have died for look like: Veets is all black, overweight, and has a bad case of dandruff and diabetes; Beamers is black and white, not so overweight, and he, too, has diabetes, as well as kidney failure and that stomach thing I mentioned before. To keep them both alive and pain-free I give them insulin injections every twelve hours. Beamers gets a subcutaneous drip of .9 percent sodium solution every other day for the kidney thing and a quarter of a tablet of Pepcid before every meal for the stomach thing. I know how cat-lady-nuts this all sounds. There's no logic to it. But as someone whose name I've long since forgotten once told me—although she was talking about people, not cats—"Love is not logical."

Or rational. A couple of months ago on Echo some friends and I were going through the various horrible things that could happen to our bodies. We'd think of something dreadful, then we'd all weigh in on whether this left life "worth living" or made it "not worth living." Would you still want to live with no legs or arms, for example? In an iron lung? Someone described a case of osteoporosis so severe you were hunchbacked and stooped with your chin inches from the sidewalk as you hobbled down the crowded streets. "Still worth living," I voted. "I'd be closer to all the cats of the world."

ROMANCE

MAURO IS NEVER getting this shirt back.

Mauro drums with me in the Manhattan Samba Group. We sleep together from time to time after we finish playing at SOB's, and we slept together last Saturday. I'm writing this like I'm cool about how casual it is, but I'm not. I just think I'm supposed to be. He's a sweet young thing and I think I'm supposed to be having fun and not taking it all so seriously, only I don't know how I feel about it. The sex is so good, though, that I try to assume a live-for-today attitude that I don't possess and tell myself that Mauro is one of my moments of glory in-between.

He left his shirt behind in my bedroom, the one he drummed in the night before. I came back that afternoon, walked in the door, and swooned. It's his smell. Actually it's half his smell and half the scent of a perfume anyone can buy, and it tricks me again and again when it comes at me from out of nowhere when I'm walking on the street. Mauro's not around, but I lift my head, sniffing, thinking, *Yes*, because I'm seeing Mauro's eyes looking down at me and starting to feel what I would normally be about to feel when I'm smelling that smell. But I'm not about to feel that now, and I end up feeling had by my longing.

I had sex with an entirely different guy only hours before having sex with Mauro. It's not as tawdry as it sounds. The earlier guy, Howard, was supposed to be The One, only he wasn't, but now I don't think I could ever have sex with Howard again, even if he offered, which he hasn't and probably won't. He dumped me for the second time—no, I think it was the third time—after sleeping with me and then went back to his previous girlfriend of three years the very next night. So I went back to Mauro, who also isn't The One. It was a desperate, last-ditch attempt to feel better.

Now I just want to wallow in the lovely, amnesia-inducing smell of Mauro. I didn't admit this to myself right away. His T-shirt was in the bedroom. At first I'd only go back there if I had a legitimate excuse, in the unlikely but already imagined event that someone might demand an explanation. While I was there I'd quickly smell his shirt, embarrassed, as if I'd be found out, even though the only way anyone would find out is if I told them. Which I did. I've had three identical conversations with three different people: my best friends, Joe and Chris, and—I'm going to hell for this—Howard. When it comes to the small but crucial questions in life, like "Hair up or hair down?" or "Is it possible to be sexy in sneakers instead of heels?" I like to take a poll.

ME: When I'm in my bedroom I smell Mauro's shirt. Is that weird?
CHRIS: No.

JOE: Yes.
HOWARD: No.

After a while I'd go back if I felt sad, like if I felt sad about Howard not being The One. Then, fuck it. Since I spend almost all my time in the living room, I picked up his shirt and put it on the couch. Now I smell him without shame as I read, write, watch TV, log on, and as I go off to sleep, intoxicated by the smell of Mauro.

I've already imagined the conversation we're going to have if he ever asks for his shirt back.

ME: Here, I bought you a new T-shirt. I'm keeping yours.
MAURO: Why?
ME: I'm not telling you. Here. Shut up.
MAURO: You're weird. [Something Mauro would say.]

This is about the extent of the conversations I have with Mauro. Who am I trying to kid? I'm trying to tell myself that it's okay that he doesn't adore me because there's no intellectual side to our relationship and that's what I really want, right? Except sometimes he calls me and sings to me on the phone for an hour and I'm lying when I say I give a damn about the intellectual side.

Mauro is twelve years younger than I am. He's Brazilian, he's beautiful, and the last thing he wants to do is to settle down. I want to settle down. But not with him. Or so I say. Then there's the T-shirt.

deαtH

I KEEP COMING BACK to death the same way I can't stop touching a sore tooth with my tongue to see if it still hurts. Death. Still terrifying? Yes. How about now? Yes. And now? Yes. Death is at the heart of the midlife crisis. "No, it's not," everybody insists. "It's about coming to terms with where you are in your life." "It's about losing your looks." Perhaps. But what's at the bottom of that? What's so scary about the middle, about all of that, if not the inescapable conclusion that the beginning is over and the end is next?

I'm flipping through a book of photographs of dead people called *Sleeping Beauty: Memorial Photography in America*, by Stanley B. Burns, M.D. Number 37 shows a man lying in his coffin, taken in 1858. We don't know his name, but the photograph is filled with clues that indicate someone cared about him very much. Except the picture is a nightmare. It makes no sense. There's all this seepage.

He's lying in a coffin lined with a delicate, snow-white, scrimlike material that surrounds his face, then trails out of the picture like a bridal veil. Someone took the time to arrange that cloth just so. Perhaps the photographer was setting up his equipment while they worked. Taking photographs was a time-consuming process in 1858. They dressed him in the best he had. You can see he's wearing an absolutely pristine, ironed white shirt. Around his neck is a tie that must have taken some-one a good twenty minutes to tie—okay, maybe it would have taken five or ten in more expert hands. The point is, it must have taken time to get it to sit just right against his neck like that. Like the shirt, it is bleached pure white and painfully, perfectly pressed.

So, they picked out a coffin. They dressed him in clothes that took a lot of trouble to prepare. They put him in. They positioned him for the picture. After they got him where they wanted him, they probably had to rearrange everything: his clothes, the tie, the coffin lining. They combed his hair. They did all this. The photographer set up his camera on the tripod. He's pulled his plates out and got everything ready. I'm guess-ing there were at least four people around while all this was going on, maybe more. Hours must have gone by.

This is what kills me. In the final photograph, as he lies there so beautifully in his white shirt and white tie against the white cloth, four tiny rivers of blood and other fluids are coming out both his nostrils and out the middle and the right side of his mouth, staining the tie. Because he's dead, his bodily fluids could not have been flowing very quickly. It must have taken hours for the stain, which is maybe four or five inches around, to spread to that size. Why, given all that activity and all that time, did no one reach over and wipe away the blood and God knows what else that was lazily making its way out of that corpse's nose and mouth? Didn't anyone have a handkerchief on them in 1858?

Why get everything just right and then not lift a finger while he oozed onto his clothes during that long and final exposure? Did they stand there, hypnotized, as the camera captured this horror movie still of love and . . . what? Fear? Or is it familiarity?

If I keep looking at this photograph, I wonder, will I become the smallest bit less terrified of my own death? I don't care how little that bit is, because I will find ways to keep adding up bits. I just want to know if it's helping, or if I'm spending what little time I have left wallowing in these panic-attack-provoking daydreams unnecessarily. I need to know that I am not wasting what's left of my midlife.

NoſtALɡiA

LOOKING BACK is like dying. Nostalgia is both a self-inflicted wound and the morphine you take for the pain—a perfect reprieve from the cold, cruel light of an untampered-with day. It hurts, but it's a good hurt. In one of his novels, Gabriel García Márquez called nostalgia a disease. Me, I can spend an hour on the playground of St. Philip Neri's on Long Island, where I went to grade school, just standing there, remembering, getting I really don't know what out of it. What does getting drunk get you? I never really feel like I can get enough. In fact, I am perpetually unsatisfied and so, like an addict who keeps going back to a drug that is never quite as good as it was the first time, I keep going back to my old school to stare and stare at two spots: the window to the classrooms and the concrete curb where I used to sit and talk to my friends. I heard the Beatles for the first time there. Someone stuck one of those plastic plugs from a pocket AM radio in my ear and my whole world changed. Gabriel García Márquez would tell me I'm going to die from this disease, and he'd be right. Nostalgia is an awareness, and regret, of the finite. It's a drug that won't make you well or young again.

This time, instead of getting on the Long Island Railroad to go back to St. Philip Neri's, I'm sitting comfortably on my big, red velvet couch with Veets and Beams—who just coughed up a furball—going through the alumni directory for Huntington High School, the school I graduated from in 1974. It lists every student from 1862 to 1995, the year I bought it. You wouldn't think it would be, but it's a page-turner. Looking at the lists of students, year by year, you can see who's alive and who's dead, who married their high school sweetheart, who moved where, who wound up staying in Huntington, and who disappeared—it's like looking inside a trunk in the town attic.

If someone has two asterisks by their name it means "Reported Deceased." One asterisk means "Address Unconfirmed." Every person up until 1899 is Reported Deceased. The oldest living graduate is Florence Thomas, now Mrs. Welch, from the class of 1918. She still lives in Huntington. And she didn't marry her high school sweetheart. I checked. No Welches in Huntington. Plus, he's either dead or they're divorced because his name isn't listed in her bio, like the names of the other spouses. There's Edward Allen from 1922, who lives in Far Rockaway and, I would guess, his sister, Kathleen Allen, now Mrs. Bollar—also not married to her high school sweetheart—who graduated in 1924 and who, like Mrs. Welch, still lives in Huntington. High-school-sweetheart-marrying is a thing of the past in the town of Huntington. It dropped off after the fifties.

There were six graduates the first year, 304 the last, and the peak year was, coincidentally, my year. Six hundred fifty-one people graduated in 1974.

18

Some families have been around since the beginning. There were graduates from the Conklin family from 1862 to 1968. The Baylises went from 1878 to 1981. The Gildersleeves lasted until 1949. Is anyone named "Gildersleeve" anymore? And then there are the Sammises. There were more graduates from the Sammis family than from any other family in Huntington. They positively ruled this town. There are Sammis graduates, often two or three at a time, between 1870 and 1977. What became of them? There were so many. Enough to ensure, you'd think, that there'd be Sammises graduating from Huntington High School forever. Did I know any of them? Did we pass each other on the street at Halloween, walking through the same leaf piles, trick-or-treating at the same houses, warning each other about which ones had boring stuff, like apples, and which had good stuff, like Snickers bars and Pixie Sticks? The Scudders are gone, too, but that's because at the end they had mostly girls, who all got married—lucky them—and took their husbands' names.

Small tragedies emerge from the lists. Every once in a while a common name pops up "Reported Deceased" across several class lists and you figure the entire family must have died together, either in a car wreck or a fire, like the Mauro brothers from the seventies, the Wheelers from the sixties, and Alfred, June, and Rudy Gumb in the fifties. I remember Don Reichbach dying when I was in high school. They told me his ex-girlfriend Melanie Seigel threw herself on his coffin at the funeral. I looked up Melanie Seigel. Dead.

The lists contain mysteries. Why were there only three graduates in 1922? There were fifty-one the year before and forty-nine the year after. An outbreak of sleeping sickness? It was going around. And why do whole classes disappear? Every single graduate of 1900, seventeen people, is listed as "Address Unconfirmed." Who abducted the entire class of 1900? No one knows where the 1906 graduates are either. The 1910 and 1912

19

grads? Gone. With the earlier years, that's kind of understand-able. It's the later years you wonder about. Starting in 1938 and lasting until 1956, almost everyone is accounted for. Then, sud-denly, single asterisks are everywhere. In 1957, 35 percent of the graduates are missing. The trend reverses in 1960. By 1967, only 4 out of 362 people have vanished. Then the class of 1968 does the most dramatic disappearing act of all—58 percent of the graduates vanish from the face of the earth. What got into the 1968 graduates? They took off, never told anyone where they were going, and never came back. It wasn't just them, it was also the people who gave birth to them. Their parents, the 1940s graduates, must have been equally restless, or they would be here to tell us the whereabouts of their children. This trend continues through the seventies.

The most recent "Reported Deceased" graduate is Beatrice A. Swezey, and she was from the class of 1994. Unlucky Beatrice is the first dead kid from the nineties. The eighties have eight. From the seventies, fifty-three people are known dead. They must have died young, before they had a chance to disappear, less irretrievably, with the rest of their classmates. If it weren't for the twenty-one people who died in 1963, the total for the six-ties, sixty-seven, wouldn't have been much higher than the sev-enties. What disaster hit the class of 1963? Vietnam? You have to go back to 1937 to find another dramatic death year. Half of that class is dead, dead, dead. World War II?

Thankfully, for the most part, Huntington High School stu-dents do not like to leave. Roughly 8,200 people who went to Huntington High School still live in Huntington and the surrounding towns, and that's just fine with me and my I-don't-like-change, I-want-to-go-back-and-find-everything-just-the-way-I-left-it heart. My brothers, Peter and Douglas, live in Huntington with their wives and children. But I can't stop thinking about the Sammises. Only a handful of them are still there, and they're all mostly beyond their childbearing years.

There's a Scott Sammis from 1970. He could have some graduates coming up if he started late. Please have started late. Please don't disappear, Sammises. I don't need another reminder that nothing lasts forever—even you, who were so all over the place in this town—and that one day I, too, will have next to my name two unrepentant, relentlessly indifferent "Reported Deceased" asterisks to scare someone else with.

poLL

F ROM A POLL OF 186 PEOPLE ON ECHO:

At what age do you think middle age begins?

("I hope it's not thirty-five," my thirty-five-year-old friend Danny answered. Jag said, "Right about . . . right about . . . no . . . right about . . . NOW!")

> Twenty-seven percent said forty.
> Twenty-two percent said forty-five.
> Nineteen percent said fifty or older.
> Sixteen percent said thirty-nine or younger.

One person said, "Middle age beings when you notice that your upholstery is hopelessly ragged and maybe even plaid, and it no longer evokes a feeling of irony." Another person, my kind of person, said, "When thoughts of death become constant." A lot of people gave this kind of answer: "Five years past whatever age I am." And a bunch of people said things like "You're only as young as you feel," but I found that answer so annoying I hit the delete key on all of them.

ROMANCE

I WENT TO A DINNER PARTY to meet the man of my dreams, and instead found the house of my dreams, where I ended up in the basement going through the boxes, books, cabinets, and bottles of an eighty-eight-year-old woman who died.

Once a week I try to go to one thing that might actually lead me to the man I will one day marry. It's comforting to think that if only I went out more I would find him—like it's all in my hands and there's reason to hope. I tell myself that if I just figure out the right place and wear the right outfit, everything will work out okay. So every week one of my friends and I go out to book parties, film screenings, art openings, and cocktail hours on terraces in the nicer parts of Brooklyn. We have just one rule. It has to be something we'd normally want to go to, unlike, say, football games, where we might meet someone who'd expect us to go to football games for the rest of our lives.

Not that I don't appreciate sports, but football—unless it's soccer—doesn't count. I wound up going alone to a book party when I couldn't reach anyone. In the courtyard, between a table stacked with books and another covered with drinks, I ran into Henry, an old friend I hadn't seen for years. He is divorced and had a broken wrist.

"How'd you break your wrist?"

"I was thrown from my horse playing polo."

I cracked up because, well, who plays polo? Henry looked offended. Still, a week later I'm invited to a dinner party at Henry's house, where he lives with his housekeeper and cook. I try to look nice because maybe the man for me is Henry, or someone else I'll meet there among the kind of people who play polo, or among people who know people who play polo. Another old friend, Barry, gives us the tour, not Henry, and I learn that Henry bought the house from the estate of the never-married Olive Huber, who was born in her parents' bedroom on the second floor in 1905 and never lived anywhere but this house from that day onward. The family took a few of her things but left the rest. Henry now sits on her chairs, sleeps in her beds, eats from her dishes, drinks from her glasses, looks at her prints and drawings on the walls, and keeps her appendix in a jar in the basement, exactly where she left it, between a bottle of Harvey's Bristol Cream and a quart of Old Taylor Kentucky Straight Bourbon Whiskey, 100 proof. Judging by the handwriting on the label, I'd say her appendix has been sitting in that house for at least seventy years. Henry's been living in the house for three years. He didn't know it was there. I hadn't been in the basement fifteen minutes before I found it. It looked like a baby flounder floating on its side, dead.

The dinner party was okay, but I called Henry afterward and asked him if I could go through Olive's things again. Two weeks later I was back in the basement, where most of Olive's personal effects are stored. My thoughts while going through the possessions of a dead woman who lived alone for most of her life: *Am I going to die alone, without enough money to feed a minimum of two cats?* (Why should a cat suffer my fate and live without a member of its own species to talk to?) *Or will I be spending time in a dry, dusty, yellow-lit courtyard in Spain?* (My image of freedom is sitting around doing nothing in a courtyard in Spain.) *Or will I actually find the man of my dreams, someone who will answer, "I'm right here," if I ever call out, frightened?* You don't need to tell me that I long to live a romance novel, not one of which, I swear to God, I've ever read. In the meantime, being in Olive and Henry's house actually makes me feel better.

It was built in 1851 by the architect Robert Voorhies and went through three owners before Olive's father, Dr. Francis Huber, bought it in 1890 for $23,000. He moved in with his wife, Viola, who played the piano—popular tunes and operetta almost exclusively—and there they raised Olive and her three brothers, Frederick, Henry, and Joseph. When Olive was in high school she broke the Olympic record for the high jump. She cleared four feet, seven and a half inches. She tried out for the Olympic track and field team in 1927, but I couldn't tell whether she made it or not. My guess is that she didn't, or there would have been a lot more clippings. There were a lot of clippings of Mildred Wiley, a member of a swim team from Boston and also a high jumper. A "lightfooted lassie," according to a local newspaper. There were also a fair number of articles from the twenties about an actress named Mabel Burke, who was described as "tall and fair, with amber-colored hair and sparkling brown eyes."

On the shelf above Olive's appendix sit several bottles of something called Dubonay Tonic (that's how it was spelled). It looks like something out of the Old West, which means it could have cocaine in it along with the alcohol. It was manufactured by the Strawberry Growers Selling Co., and the label reads:

For Health's Sake. Dosage: Wine Glass Full 3 Times a Day Morning Noon and Night After Meals. Alcohol 20%. Contents 16 ounces. A Natural Palatable Tonic Indicated as a Reliable Stimulant and System Builder.

There was another old Ball jar with something that I thought was a gray-colored new potato—until I found the appendix. Now I'm thinking it's probably not a new potato. Olive saved everything. I found telephone numbers of hat blockers and handymen and a stack of magazines dating from 1895 that belonged to her brother Henry and that can only be described as softcore pornography, called *Sarony's Living Pictures*. At the age of sixty-seven, Olive retired from Hunter College, where she had been a professor and chair of the department of physiology and health for forty years. She died on May 14, 1993.

Olive didn't change much about the house while she lived here. Neither has Henry. I found a set of plans for renovations done in Olive's father's time, and another set from the 1960s, along with pictures of Olive and her friends and relatives in the same rooms I had wandered through with my fellow guests. As far as I can tell the place hasn't been altered much, just restored and kept up. Olive and Henry are my kind of people, the kind who go from room to room, looking at the floor, the plasterwork, fingering the paintings and chairs, thinking, *Still here, still here, still here.* What is it about opening drawers and finding the same buttons, matches, fuses, old birthday cards, and other odds and ends that makes me feel so protected and not, as other people might feel, buried? When I drink out of a cup that I've been drinking out of for thirty years, it's a death-defying act. I feel permanent and invincible. *I'll be all right*, I think, *everything will be all right, as long as nothing changes, as long as I can keep drinking out of this cup here.*

Every room in Olive and Henry's house is a lovely, deep,

27

unchanged dream: floor-to-ceiling windows that look out on a maple tree and an ivy-filled garden, radiator iron molded into leaves and vines, etched-glass doors that separate the main rooms, and the original wood and plaster moldings along the door frames and around the ceilings. There are two fireplaces on each floor, but Henry never uses them. "The fireplaces are too small," he says. Olive's mother's piano sat unplayed for three years until I pulled up a chair and did my best with a Scott Joplin rag (which wasn't too good, because last Christmas I sold my piano, which I never played much to begin with). When I called Henry to ask him if I could come back, he asked, "Do you date?" He wanted to know whether I had an easy time of it, meeting people. "Yes, I date," I told him. "No, I don't have an easy time of it." During lunch, prepared and served by his live-in cook (this is the first thing I'm going to do when I make my millions, boy—hire a cook), he asked, "What did you think of the woman who was sitting at your table?" He was talking about the banker who was at his dinner party the week before. "Henry," I said. "She's a banker."

The next week Henry went out with the banker. "It wasn't all that fun," he told me later. "I don't think I'll go out with her again. Want to come over tomorrow night and play Risk?" "No," I answered. What's the point? I doubt he was even think-ing of me "that way," but I couldn't even fantasize about get-ting involved with someone who, given the choice, chose the banker. Then I thought of a love spell my friend Chris taught me when we were both fourteen. You write the name of the boy you want on a piece of paper, fold it up, then burn it in the flame of a dark red candle. If you do everything just right, the boy you love will love you back. Since then, I've watched a lot of names blacken and curl in these tiny, blue-orange fires. One day I changed the ritual. Instead of writing down a name, I wrote, "I give up. You choose. Just let me recognize him when

I meet him." I was worried that the man of my dreams might be right in front of me and that I was missing him. So now it occurs to me: doesn't it make sense that the man for me might be equally clueless?

cats

6:30 A.M. Beamers jumps up on my chest and wakes me up.

6:33 A.M. Veets bats my face with a paw, nails extended.

6:38 A.M. Beams sits behind my head and starts treadling.

6:43 A.M. Beamers jumps up on my chest again.

6:44 A.M. Beamers drools on my arm.

6:49 A.M. One of them digs, continuously, for five minutes straight, in the kitty litter.

6:49 A.M. I can smell it.

6:50 A.M. Beamers jumps up on the coffee table, lands on a magazine, and slides off the other side.

6:52 A.M. Veets jumps on my chest from across the living room floor.

6:53 A.M. I think I slept for a minute.

6:54 A.M. Veets jumps on my chest, misses, digs his nails into my chest to stop from falling, falls anyway, dragging his nails down my chest.

6:55 A.M. Veets starts eating from the garbage. I try to remember if I threw out anything poisonous.

6:56 A.M. Beamers picks up a Ping-Pong ball and cries with the Ping-Pong ball stuck in his mouth and I think it's because it's too big for his mouth and he's crying for me to help him get it out before he chokes to death and I have to rush him to the hospital but then he drops it.

6:57 A.M. Veets and Beams charge up onto my desk. (Pigeon in the window.)

6:57 A.M. I watch them because what if they get cut to ribbons crashing through the window to get the pigeon and I have to rush them to the hospital?

6:59 A.M. Veets starts gagging. I watch him to see if it's just a furball or something worse and I have to rush him to the hospital, but it turns out to be a furball. "Gack. Gack. Gack." (Their furball-throwing-up noise.)

6:59 A.M. Beams starts eating the leaves from a plant, which makes him vomit.

6:59 A.M. I push him away from the plant.

6:59 A.M. Now Veets is eating a leaf.

7:00 A.M. *When is someone going to love me who isn't a cat?*

7:01 A.M. I get up.

work

I STARTED ECHO ten years ago when I wasn't middle-aged and when I still had a little money in the bank. Since then it's taken every penny I've ever saved and pushed me into growing negative numbers, which gives me anxiety attacks whenever I think about it, which is, of course, often—*Clean slate, clean slate, clean slate* (it's something I dream about). I worry about my twilight years, but the fact remains that I love Echo. I love everyone in it, including the people I don't actually like very much.

I'll explain. Every day a few thousand overeducated, pushy, and—considering how pushy they are—entirely too sensitive New Yorkers, all of whom have either been in therapy at one time or another or should be, log on to Echo to talk about books, movies, TV, politics, and so forth. That's the official story. They're really logging on to talk about themselves and about their next favorite subject after that—other people on Echo. Everyone keeps up with what's going on, or not going on, in everyone else's life by participating in various conversations where, regardless of the supposed topic under discussion, the real subject is How I Fucked Up Today, or Famous Fuckups from My Past, or That's Nothing Compared to What a Fuckup You Are, or I Hate Myself. It's all in the subtext. It's like when you're falling in love, you could be talking about Malraux, Sartre, and Camus, and what you're really saying, no matter what you're saying, is "I love you." This is New York. We're miserable and cranky and proud of it, and this is the undercurrent in everything we talk about.

Now, although the self-recrimination and self-loathing are genuine, reading about everyone else's lives is half the fun. "It's better than TV," I frequently hear. There's no exaggerating the voyeuristic pleasure of cyberspace. On Echo you get to watch everyone screw up on a daily—or, for some, minute-by-minute—basis and from this you can see where you fit on the loser curve. "Oh, I'm not as big an idiot as he is," or "Oh, God, I'm worse." What's more, Echo, unlike TV, lets you talk back. That's when the fun really begins. It's like stopping and interacting with a traffic accident instead of having to crane your neck as you drive slowly by.

For example, a couple of weeks ago a woman on Echo who used to work as a restaurant hostess admitted to seating fat people at the back of the restaurant where their presence wouldn't offend the other diners. God, were the people on Echo all over that one. "I was only kidding," she responded defensively—an obvious lie, and it just made matters worse. *What was she thinking?* you wonder. We have a number of ongoing discussions on Echo, all variations on "I'm Embarrassed to Admit It, but . . ." Everyone loves to confess things because frequently the things we are so ashamed of turn out to be so common, such as how long we'd go without bathing if we didn't

33

have to go to work or out on a date, or how no one's finished *Gravity's Rainbow* (except for the people who brag about having read it many times). And you'd be surprised how many people believe "I Think I Love You," by the Partridge Family, is a really great song. Coming clean brings relief. The former restaurant hostess must have believed that underneath, we were all just like her, and that a lot of other people were going to come forward with "Me too!" She must have also thought that we are all thin.

Instead, the people on Echo were bonding over not being her. E-mail went back and forth, fast and furious: "Did you see what she just said?" "What are you going to say back?" Everyone logged on to watch the latest developments. She squirmed. They pulled up chairs and ate popcorn. It's not that they hated her. If she went away they'd miss her. Echo's like a small town. We have our losers, but they're *our* losers. If people left whenever there was a conflict or misunderstanding, there'd be no fireworks. Where's the fun in that?

When the former restaurant hostess e-mailed us for advice, I thought of a continuing conversation we have on Echo called "What Would Mary Do?" When we get into a difficult spot, we try to figure out how Mary Richards from *The Mary Tyler Moore Show* would have handled it. Mary, we decided, would have told her to hang in there. "Ride it out," we advised. "Don't run away from your problems." She took our advice, and we all moved on. That's us—the dysfunctional family Echo. I agree with my friend Marianne: people are mean sometimes because they're disappointed. At least on Echo there's the entertainment value. If only it were more profitable. I've got my twilight years to think about.

MUSIC

TALENTED PEOPLE have it so easy. From somewhere over the rainbow, something comes to you just like that, without all those endless rounds of try/fail, try/fail, try/fail that kick back only the most pathetically small successes. I'm not what you would call a natural drummer. In fact, for the longest time, I sucked. If you ask Ivo, the guy who runs the Manhattan Samba Group, I still suck. Thankfully, I've discovered that talent isn't the most important thing in the world. If I hold on until the bitter end, I get good at whatever. Well, not good, exactly; good enough, rather. So I tend not to give up on things. Ever. I'd make a most excellent stalker.

The minute I picked up the drum, though, I wanted to be on the red-yellow-green glowing stage of SOB's every Saturday, being loved and desired by Brazilians right now, right this very second. But I had to wait. Ivo tells us when we're ready. But I couldn't wait. Couldn't he see that I didn't have all the time in the world? I had to get up there. So I bought a drum to practice on in between our weekly classes. The Brazilians call it a *caixa*. We call it a snare. It hangs from a strap across your chest and you play it with drumsticks, not your hands.

I went back to my apartment to play, but it made a sound like a gun going off, a .44 Magnum to be exact, and I had to admit to myself that this was not going to work. I'd have had to bribe everyone in the building to put up with it, and then start on the one next door. I had to find another place to practice. Someplace very noisy, I was thinking, someplace where no one could accuse me of disturbing the peace because, in the place I chose, there'd be no peace.

I headed outside. Half an hour later I found it: a construction site on the Hudson River. There were jackhammers, trucks, and backhoes all over the place—an all-noise-all-the-time spot. Unfortunately, there was also a whole river society, and they were very tight: runners, walkers, dog people, people on the benches. And while they may have come to accept the construction noise, they were not going to put up with the sound of a .44 Magnum going off, over and over. And then there was the matter of, as I mentioned before, me sucking. "You suck," they yelled at me as they ran by. *Shut up.* I didn't yell back because I really do have a powerful timid streak. I am so ashamed of my complete failure as a take-no-shit New Yorker. People from Kansas walk all over me. The construction workers were on my side. "Hey, tough girl," they shouted to encourage me. "Sounding good."

When I really got going, though, I was alone on the river and there was no stopping me. There were no people in my world, only the drum. I was aware of the sunlight because it made me squint, the wind because it made my hair go in my mouth, and that slightly dead smell that salt water gives off. I love that smell. I smelled it as a child growing up by the

Long Island Sound. I would squat down in the sand, looking for fish in the small pools of water left when the tide goes out. It was such a sweet loneliness. To hell with the everyone's-a-music-critic river society. Tourists took pictures of me as they strolled by.

After a couple of months of practicing, oblivious to all life forms on the Hudson, an incredible racket—which, incredibly, wasn't coming from me—broke through my consciousness. I don't know how long the sound had been building up, but it came to me so suddenly it was like coming out of a coma into a banging and clanking, too-bright world. I looked up. Oh God. Now, *this* was true bliss. My construction worker friends were accompanying me. Using whatever pieces of pipes and tools they could find, and with the biggest, most eager and affectionate smiles on their faces, they were drumming on their trucks and barrels, wailing away and making as much noise as they possibly could, trying to match the samba swing that I was desperately trying to bang out on my *caixa*. I will never forget their faces. They'd just given me the best possible present and they knew it. They knew it. It felt as good as anything I've felt on the stage at SOB's, or anyplace else.

On the morning of Halloween they stood around me in a semicircle and asked if I was going to drum in the Halloween parade. I was surprised, first that they even knew there was going to be a parade, and second, that they knew drumming was a big part of it. "That's what I've been practicing for all these months," I told them. Well, they were going to be there. They'd been rooting for me for months and they were going to fucking be there. "Fuckin' A," I answered. (A popular expression from my Long Island childhood. I can't get rid of it.) I had just racked up a moment of in-between glory.

ʄantaʄy

I FANTASIZE ABOUT GOING up to Ruben Blades, who is having lunch at an outdoor restaurant in the Village. We have the following conversation.

ME: Twenty years ago I took your photograph for Reuters and I was so distracted by you that the photographs didn't come out and they never hired me again. Come to think of it, I never worked as a professional photographer again.

RUBEN: You're making this up.

ME: No. The writer was my friend Aly Sujo and he asked me to take the pictures while he interviewed you.

RUBEN: But you look twenty now. What, did you take those pictures when you were an infant?

ME: (Blushing. Stammering just a little.) Oh. Thank you.

No. I'm forty-two. Anyway, I just wanted to say I've never forgotten that, or you. I'm sorry for interrupting your lunch.

I walk away. He follows me. We fall in love and get married. I wear a Vera Wang wedding gown.

beauty

IF YOU'RE MIDDLE-AGED, your looks are going. Sometimes I couldn't care less about this, which is great—freedom! Take makeup. I'm down to practically no makeup at all. I just can't be bothered. Foundation, blush, eyeshadow, eyeliner, mascara, eyebrow pencil, lipstick. What a production.

Actually, it's not that I can't be bothered. It's that I'm really not bothered by how my face looks without makeup. However, the things that do bother me take over, they become everything, which is not great, because the kinds of things I obsess about are bigger-deal things, and there's not a lot I can do about them without major surgery.

Like my stomach. I have a stomach. It sticks out as much as the stomach of a woman six months pregnant. "You don't have a stomach," my friends tell me. "You're womanly." But then I get a glimpse of myself in a dressing room mirror. (What is it about the mirrors in department stores that strips the veil away?) What I see isn't womanly. It's sad.

Everywhere I go I compare stomachs. If I'm on the street I'm looking at other women's stomachs. I have to see if theirs protrude as much as mine. *Doesn't. Doesn't. Doesn't. Doesn't.* I've tried every exercise in the book to reduce this . . . this thing. I look down at my stomach and it's like a separate thing. *Get it off me!* I was up to five hundred sit-ups a day without achieving any noticeable difference, when someone told me that it wasn't that sit-ups don't work, it was that I wasn't doing them the "right way." So I learned the "right way" and felt the difference immediately. When you do sit-ups the "right way," the muscles under the fat, which doesn't go down even a little bit, become as hard as a rock.

I also obsess about my teeth. The same teeth didn't bother me when I was twenty. What were a few crooked teeth when everything else was taut, springy, and on the way up, up, up? Well, they bother me now. Everything matters now. Take shoes. For most of my adult life I've worn sneakers. Given the choice between style or comfort, I chose comfort because, well, I could get away with it. I wasn't thinking that. I didn't have to think at all. I was young and cute and, sneakers or heels, it didn't make a difference. I didn't care because I didn't have to care. Now I feel like I have to make an effort.

Last summer I was showing my friend Liz pictures of people on Echo that I've been collecting over the years. I found one of myself from ten years earlier. I stared and stared. For ten minutes I stared. Only ten years ago. Such a small amount of time.

After I came out of my trance Liz said, "Okay. Explain."

"I used to look a lot better," I told her.

She immediately launched into the you-still-look-good argument. But it wasn't that I didn't still look good. It's that I didn't look *that* good. Sitting there on that couch, looking at a decade-old photograph, I knew it, and now I will always know it. You can't take that kind of awareness back. Thirty-two—looking good. Forty-two—you still look good. Fifty-two—not bad for fifty-two? Sixty-two—what? There's just no getting around it. My looks are going, and they will keep on going until no one looks at me with that liking-what-they-see expression again. I know. Beauty is in the eye of the beholder, and it's what's inside that counts, blah, blah, blah. But the subset of beholders who will stick around long enough to find out what's inside is shrinking. Don't tell me that looks aren't everything. I know. But they're not nothing. What I want to know is, will I always care? It's like quitting smoking. I remember thinking I'd rather keep smoking and die of cancer than spend the rest of my life tormented day after day by the desire for just one more puff. But the desire did fade.

Am I going to spend the rest of my life tormenting myself, considering the endless corrections I could make just for one last looking-good look?

Yes.

Nope, no transcendence here. Now I have to decide (because I can't afford both): Should I spend thousands of dollars for veneers for my teeth, and pray that my dazzling smile will distract from my cartoon stick-out stomach? Or should I go for liposuction, because with a flat, lovely stomach like my future stomach, who's going to look at my teeth? I can't make up my mind.

beatrice richter

PEOPLE IN THEIR TWILIGHT YEARS have got to know something I don't. I want to find out before there's nothing left of them but boxes of crumbling artifacts or an appendix sitting in a jar in someone's attic or basement. What if it's nothing? I found a great quote in *TV Guide*. It was in an article about a documentary on romance in the twilight years. Some guy recovering from open-heart surgery said, "It seems to me that life should have greater meaning than it actually does." I find that both frightening and comforting. It would make my life of drumming, cats, and staring at pictures of dead people no more or less meaningful than anyone else's.

So I have a few questions for the people who have been around for a long time. Do the petty cares, about teeth and stomachs for example, fade? Does the idea of death become any less terrifying? I want them to sum it all up for me. In the end, what really matters?

Beatrice Richter was born October 1, 1915, in New York City. The first time we talked on the phone, Beatrice cried when she started talking about her special-education students. She went from premed studies to business school to working for the Roosevelt campaign to being chief of histology at Mount Sinai, but she had little to say about any of that. She wanted to talk about her students. "Their parents still call me even though I've been retired for more than twenty years." "It's a wonderful life," I tell her. She keeps a clay sculpture that she made of a former pupil on a table next to her couch. It's a boy around eleven. His eyes are closed. I think that's because it's harder to make open eyes in clay.

In 1939, and even though Beatrice had had a recent bout of undulant fever—so called because of its characteristic symptom of afternoon temperature spikes—which left her with stringy hair, yellow skin, and her five-foot-eight-inch frame reduced to 112 pounds, Frank Richter fell in love with her on sight when they danced to Tommy Dorsey's band at the Pennsylvania Hotel. They married on December 20, 1942. Beatrice had to spend their honeymoon alone because Frank had enlisted and went straight into training. They had three children and a happy marriage, until Frank's death in 1993.

When I talked to Beatrice, her brother had died just a few weeks before. He was ninety-five years old and had been her guiding light. When they were kids, he taught her how to dance, swim, and play the saxophone, and when he died she broke down and wept. "It was the only funeral I ever really cried at," she told me. "Not even my husband."

Now she is leaving the house she has lived in for the past forty-five years to move into a Lutheran-run retirement village in Allentown, Pennsylvania. She is afraid. For the first time in her life.

Are you old?

I just started to feel old. I got past eighty-two, and all of a sudden I found it hard to shop, to cook. Up until then I was not old. I'm still not really old. But I never minded eating alone before.

I eat alone most of the time and I don't mind, I think in response to what Beatrice has said. *Will that change for me, too, when I get older?*

What are the main differences between the young you and the you now?

I don't ever remember being a kid. My mother put me in the first grade when I was five years old and she told them I was six. When they found out, I got up and walked out. I was five years old and I crossed Lexington Avenue, I crossed Park Avenue, then I walked from 108th Street to 111th Street and said to my mother, "You lied." I wouldn't go back until the next year, when I really was six.

Did you have a midlife crisis?

No. I was too busy.

How do you feel when you see your body in the mirror?

Everyone tells me I look wonderful. I just lost thirty pounds. I'm pleased with myself. I've shrunk a bit. We all shrink.

She's gone from five-eight to about five-four. She is pretty, but a little shaky. Her head trembles.

What scares you?

Everything. Nothing ever scared me before, but when I saw all the furniture going out of here my heart went. It was all I could do to keep from crying. My mother's heirlooms. Her din-ing room set. They are out of my life. This whole house will be out of my life.

My heart went, just listening to her.

Is there anything that no longer frightens you?
Animals. I was bitten by a police dog when I was nine. He took a chunk about two or three inches wide out of me. I had a job injecting mice and rats when I was twenty-one. It scared me. I had to grit my teeth to do it. But I did it. I'm still not completely comfortable around animals.

Is there anything you no longer care about?
I never longed for anything that wasn't possible. I could bitch about a lot of things, but it wouldn't do me any good. I still care about everything.

You are addressing someone you care about, someone young. Please finish this sentence: "If you only knew . . ."
. . . how wonderful life could be. Just don't be afraid. Now I'm afraid. Why did I become so afraid? I did something wrong. What did I do wrong? You have to make every minute of life count. Why did I become afraid of the unknown?

She cries and asks me again, "What did I do wrong?" I want to make her feel better. "Nothing," I tell her. "Nothing. It's amazing that you were never this afraid before."

Fast-forward to your deathbed. You're saying good-bye to friends and loved ones. Is there anything you've left unsaid that you'd like to say while you still have the chance?
I love them all, all the time. I'm proud of my children. One is a judge, one is a professor, and one is an editor at a major newspaper. Live a good life. Just don't be afraid. You're all afraid.

She cries again. She asks me if I'm afraid. "All the time," I tell her.

Which of your possessions would you hope will not be thrown out?

Nothing. I'm trying to get rid of everything. I threw out everything I was saving. That scares me.

What would you like to experience one last time?

I'd like to see what happens to my grandchildren. You watch your kids, you get to see how it all turns out. I'd like to experience that with my grandchildren. But I probably won't. I wonder how far I'll get.

Looking back on it all, what will you miss the most? What are your most favorite things in the world? On a day-to-day basis, what are the things that give you pleasure?

It took a long time for her to come up with an answer. She had trouble thinking of things that made her happy.

Clean sheets, as long as I'm not the one washing them. Exercising. I'm pleased with myself that I have enough energy to get down on the floor and move. NPR, my Jackson roses, chocolate. I can't eat my favorite foods anymore. A problem in my esophagus. I don't play records anymore. I love British comedies. *Keeping Up Appearances* is my favorite. Sitcoms bother me. I don't like *Seinfeld*. People don't do anything in their lives.

Who will you miss the most?

My children. My husband. He was a sweet, wonderful man. He was gorgeous. He looked like Jimmy Stewart. I'm mad at him, though. I helped him grow old but he isn't here to help me. I don't know what I'm going into. Who knows what death will have in store?

Was it worth it? Why?

Yes. I did a good job. The kids I taught are still alive and they still talk about me. But they have Alzheimer's now. They're in their fifties. They didn't used to live so long, but they're living longer now and they are developing Alzheimer's-like symptoms and no one knows why. I see wonderful, wonderful people wearing out. I'm a little worried about living into my nineties. And wearing out. I didn't used to feel old.

The first time I got off the phone with Beatrice I couldn't sit still. I wanted to see her. I want her to be okay, although, thanks to Sherwin Nuland, I now know that few people are okay in the end. But I told her it would probably be okay, and I didn't want it to be an out-and-out lie. If Beatrice gets through it, maybe I will, too. By "get through it" I mean not spending the last years in a total panic. As if dying isn't bad enough.

I called her three weeks after she had moved to Allentown. She seemed happier. But when she said, "You see a lot of walkers and wheelchairs. I realize by now that that has to be," she sounded a little defeated. Last week I drove down with her daughter to visit her. She told me she likes the Lutherans. "But you have to dress up for dinner." Her arms swept down to indicate her outfit. "I can't go like this." She was wearing olive-green silk slacks and an embroidered T-shirt. That counts as casual dressy for me. "And there aren't any normal people." Normal people? "Everyone was a very important person when they were working. No one was a secretary." Beatrice was raised in a Jewish household that was not the most observant, yet she hopes she can find more than the three Jews she'd found so far. "Why'd you pick this place?" I asked. She'd been coming to Allentown for twenty years to visit her son the professor, who lives here with his family. So it's familiar.

Beatrice didn't cry once when I went to see her. She refused to complain no matter how hard I tried to get her to, and I did try. Because I thought that's what you're supposed to do: get it all out. But Beatrice Richter is determined to be brave. She was a gracious host, who walked with me through a graveyard and down the main street of Allentown. She asked me to read to her what was on the graves. I think she was just being polite.

cats

NOT TOO LONG AGO I walked into the veterinarian's office where I take Veets and Beams and the person behind the counter called out, "Ladies and gentlemen, guard your cats! Any cat that comes near that woman gets diabetes!" Even though it was obvious he was kidding—and how do people think you get diabetes, anyway?—everyone visibly shrank. They pulled their cat carriers close and watched me. Always the unfailing blame-accepter, I probably looked guilty.

It started with Beamers. Beamers practically lived at the vet's. I must have been bringing him there every two or three months for the first few years of his life. I was a wreck. We all were—me, Veets, and Beams. A year or so before he was finally diagnosed with diabetes they told me that once again they'd have to keep him overnight for observation, and I just lost it. It upsets the cat to be away from home, it upsets the cat who is left alone, and it upsets me. I started shaking and was about to cry when the vet snapped at me. "Listen"—if it were a movie he would have slapped me—"you have to calm down. You're scaring your cat." I looked over at the shivering Beams— he was still such a little thing—and I realized he was right. I composed myself, and I swear this had an immediate calming effect on Beamers. He was terrified because I was terrified. After that I didn't have to compose myself as often. Once they figured out Beams was diabetic, the number of his vet visits went down to about two a year.

Diabetes in cats is controlled pretty much the way diabetes in humans is controlled. You check their insulin levels by sticking a special strip of plastic into their urine, you wait thirty seconds while it changes color, and then you match that color against the colors on a chart. After a few months Beamer's strips were coming out dark brown, indicating a high level of glucose. Everything else about him seemed okay, but the strips were consistently dark brown, so I raised his insulin. It didn't help. The strips continued to come out dark brown, almost black, and in only fifteen seconds. I decided it was the strips. The strips were bad. I came up with a test. I'd stick one in Veets's urine and if it came out positive I'd know I was right. Veets tested positive. *I knew it*, I thought. I called the vet. "The strips aren't bad," he told me. "Bring Veets in." Veets was diagnosed with diabetes.

ME: How can that be?
VET: I don't know.
ME: But he's not related to Beamers. How can they both have diabetes?
VET: Amazing, isn't it?

Pause.

ME: I didn't even know until a few months ago that cats could even get diabetes, and now you're telling me I have two diabetic cats?
VET: Yeah.

I was not getting nearly enough sympathy, damn it. Because I downplayed diabetic-cat ownership. Here's what's involved. First, you leave your cat at the vet's for days while they test a variety of insulins in order to find the right one, the right amount, and the right number of times a day to inject it. By the time they're done you're out a thousand dollars. And it doesn't end there. Sometimes the insulin stops working and they have to start all over again: different insulin, different amounts, different frequency. Another thousand bucks. Then there are the glucose strips. It's better to catch their urine midstream, while it's fresh, rather than sticking the strip into a pool of slightly less-than-fresh urine. This means you have to hold the plastic strip under your cat's butt while he pees, for the love of God. Cats don't like this any more than you do, so they soon become expert at going to the bathroom while you're out or when you're asleep. Your life revolves around catching your cat peeing. Whatever you're doing—watching TV, reading— you always keep half an eye on your cats because you have to be ready at any moment to jump up and stick a glucose strip under their butt. Sometimes you jump up and it's a false alarm: they were only changing their sleeping position. Sometimes you panic. You fumble with the container and you can't get the strip out in time. Sometimes, I'm convinced, they're just trying to see how many times they can make you jump up. I'm sure that after I go to bed Veets and Beams laugh and laugh and laugh—while peeing, of course—about how many times they faked me out that day. In any case, for the rest of the cats' lives—and they can live long lives, if you're vigilant—it's injections and urine tests.

Sometimes you need to test their blood. Urinalysis is crude. Humans don't even use urine tests anymore, because blood tests are more accurate. To draw a cat's blood you have to get the cat to sit still while you prick the vein that runs along his ear, and then you somehow have to convince a bleeding cat not to move, so that you can maneuver his head to get his blood onto a different and very narrow plastic strip for a different color chart match-up. And now I had to do all this work, times two.

I looked at the vet and raised my voice.

ME: What are the odds of two cats adopted on two separate occasions both turning out to be diabetic??

He understands that he needs to express some empathy here, and he tries.

VET: Astronomical!

But I couldn't accept it. I was sure the vet had made a mistake. *Aha*, I think. *I'll test my own urine. If I come up positive it has to mean the strips are bad and the vet's tests are wrong and I don't have two diabetic cats after all*. I went home and peed. Negative. I was clean. So now I lie in wait for two—*two*—cats to pee. And while I wouldn't have thought it possible, the experience made me even more unnaturally close to Veets and Beams.

deAtH

THE AGE AT WHICH most men commit suicide: seventy-five and older. For women, the suicide rate peaks between forty-five and fifty-four.

I guess midlife is harder for women. It seems like I'm not alone in my rush toward the inevitable. Although death is the one thing I don't want to hurry up. I'd like to announce right here and now that when it comes to keeping me alive, I want heroic measures taken. Even if I'm colorless, bedsore-ridden, with my limbs and fingers and toes all impossibly curled back up into myself, I could be the one in katrillion who wakes back up, so please, keep me going.

When women—excuse me, middle-aged women—want to die, they use a gun: 40.5 percent of them do, to be exact. Poison comes next, at 26.1 percent, then hanging or strangulation, and after that, jumping from high places. Middle-aged women are most likely to blow their brains out on a Monday, between noon and six P.M., least likely to do so on a Saturday, and, if they're not married, they're going to pull the plug on a Monday in the spring. New York, happily, has one of the lowest suicide rates in the country. Nevada, New Mexico, Arkansas, and Arizona top the I've-had-it charts. Incidentally, the experts can't decide whether cats kill themselves. One says they can't because they don't have a mature concept of death, whatever that is. Another said that the "suicidal motive could manifest itself in many indirect, covert, and unconscious ways, and, therefore, animals can commit suicide." I don't know. Cats get depressed. I look over at Veets and Beams. Oh, God, I hate myself. My first thought was about the thousands of dollars I've spent keeping them alive. "Better not," I say to them. "Feed us," I'm sure they'd respond.

Me? As long as I have TV, I'm hanging in there. If the show is good, I am as content watching TV as I am doing anything else. I'm that shallow. I admit it. So yeah, I can see myself happily watching TV at ninety, just me and my cats. Sad, I know. It goes back to my childhood. I was sick all the time and I spent the first five years of my life largely alone. As a result, I am perfectly fine with solitude. I can entertain myself for hours and hours, just me and my head.

Look, I'm not saying it's ideal, but I would call watching TV a life.

fAMiLY

WHERE DID I GET my fascination with death? Mom. The whole time I was growing up it seemed like the only people she spoke glowingly and lovingly about were dead. The live people were nice, but the dead people were nicer. They were always kinder, funnier, and prettier, and because I was a kid and literal-minded, I got the idea that all the best people were dead. My mother's mother, Gertrude Eugenia Armstrong (everyone called her Daisy), was the best one of all. Daisy died when she was forty-seven, on August 6, 1951, at 6:40 A.M., five years before I was born and seven days before my mother's seventeenth birthday. Cause of death: coronary thrombosis. I've read that children who lose their parents never get over it. My mother was so convincing that I've never gotten over Daisy's death, either. I miss her, too. Except in my case I miss the image of a person and not the actual person, and this has become the story of my life.

After Daisy's death my mother went to live with her father, Walter, who had left when my mother was three. Two years later he died of the exact same thing while walking along the street, on his way to his job at Con Edison. Walter had never missed a day of work in his life. The day he died a coworker joked, "Oh, Walter isn't in today. He must be dead." My mother was the one who went to the mortuary to identify his body, even though there were plenty of adult relatives around who could have done it. He was the last of her immediate family to go. Her grandmother Jennie had died of a heart problem when my mother was eleven.

I have a picture of Daisy in her wedding dress on my wall in the living room, next to my desk. I keep it there because I was raised with heaven and hell and angels, and even though I don't believe any of it, sometimes I pray to Daisy to help me just in case (1) I'm wrong, because I so frequently am, and (2) she cares to, and (3) she is in a position to do so. I've also got a picture of my great-grandfather Claudius "Claude" Dennis Corke, and I ask him for help, too. I look like Claude and I hope the resemblance will make him more sympathetic to my woes.

Daisy was beautiful. And delicate. You can see it in the wedding photograph even though you can't see much. She had a heart condition and she wasn't supposed to climb steps. Though delicate, she was also determined. I wrote to the hospital where she died and was told that she graduated from high school at an early age, even though she'd had to stay in bed as a child because of her heart and missed three years of school. She was also told never to have kids, but after three full-term pregnancies that ended in death (two sons were born dead, and one lived only a week), she had my mother, Jeanne Lorraine, when she was thirty.

When my mother was ten one of her aunts came to take her dog, Snowy, away from her, so that a cousin could give Snowy to a girl he was proposing to. Daisy didn't stop her. It's the only story my mother's ever told me in which Daisy, who was adored by all, is anything less than perfect. I'm not sure what a woman who wouldn't stop that aunt from taking Snowy away can do for me and my woes. My mother insists that no one stood up to this aunt. I think my mother grew up protecting the alternately determined and delicate Daisy, and I think she's protecting her still.

Though abandoned by Walter, Daisy never married again. She fell in love one more time, but the Church wouldn't give her an annulment. She lived alone with my mother for the rest of her life, working at one secretarial job after another until July 13, 1951, a month before she died, when she was admitted to Pilgrim Psychiatric Center on Long Island with a diagnosis of involutional psychosis, depressed type. She was "hallucinating, withdrawn and mildly assaultive," her records state. "Mildly assaultive," my friend Matt translates for me, means she didn't want to be there and she struggled. I'm glad to hear she fought back, but also sad because it means she was scared and wanted to go home.

Her records don't say much else. Nobody wrote down her thoughts or her feelings and they don't say what her hallucinations were. It's been almost fifty years and my mother still doesn't like to talk about it. I wish I could see Daisy's room. And the people who were with her during her last days—what were they like? After the initial shock of being committed against her will, did my grandmother think she was going to at long last get some help and some rest? Or was she frightened until the very end, never quite accepting this final disappointment?

I have always felt a connection to Daisy, because I was born with a hole in my heart. Having a hole in your heart was a much bigger deal in 1956 than it is now. The doctors told my mother that I might not make it, and you can imagine what this did to her. She lost people all over the place because of heart trouble, one every five years to be exact, and now that she was twenty-one years old it was time to lose another. The hole closed, I lived, but during those crucial, formative years, I believe my mother communicated to me that I would be dead soon, so naturally I was curious about what that meant. Later, with all her stories of loss and the wonderful Daisy's failing heart, I romanticized death. I was given the sense, which has never left me, that I've missed something, and that everything good was dead and gone before I was born. It keeps drawing me back into the past. My whole life I've never looked more than a year or two into the future.

My mother likes to tell me that she concentrated on making me independent more than anything else. She says she did this because she never felt independent herself. I don't think she ever had the luxury of a dependent moment in her life.

Her father left when she was three and her mother wasn't supposed to climb steps. Daisy and Jeanne never had a chance. Daisy wasn't strong enough to stand up to the Church or that aunt, so she worked harder than she should have and without any hope for the man of her dreams. And the little girl who was my mother had to be strong for Daisy, and didn't have anyone to tell her aunt to get her own goddamned dog.

I did, in fact, grow up to be very independent, but with bizarro side effects. I pray to dead people. It makes me feel better. Whether it helps or not, I like having these pictures of my dead relatives near me. Photographs of Daisy and Claude hang next to me as I type. I stare and stare, and try to see them as living people who, like me, were hit with the awareness that the only forever they'd know was forever unrealized dreams. Daisy—whose help I want the most, maybe because she lived without love for so long she might understand what I'm going through—is the hardest one to imagine alive. She's not looking into the camera in that wedding photo. And the colors are not like colors from life; they're old-photograph colors. There simply isn't enough information to conjure her up. But if somehow I can, I think, I won't disappear so completely either. It's a tiny resurrection, but if I string enough of them together, maybe they will add up to something. I decide that visiting Daisy's grave will help.

"Where is Daisy buried, Mom?"

"I don't remember."

"Where did she die?"

"Somewhere in Queens, I don't know. Why are you asking me this?"

I don't want to tell her the real reason. *Because I want Daisy to rescue me, Mom.*

Noſtalgia

I MADE IT TO the Veterans' Day parade at the very end. The
skies were still spitting rain but the real storm was over and
the last marchers were coming around the corner and stopping
in front of Madison Square Park. All the drummers except one
were girls, I noticed. I couldn't help checking, even though that
wasn't why I was there and I felt bad for taking the time. I
always get to the parade late, but always in the nick of time to
smile weakly at the aging soldiers wandering around, looking
mostly lost. A pale and unsteady veteran, standing five feet
from me, collapsed a few minutes into the ceremony. "We're
pulling out," one of his comrades called as they put him in a
chair and carried him away.

I clapped for every person they introduced, even the mayor,
because I didn't want a single gesture to be interpreted as dis-
respect. I wore a skirt, which I almost never do. I thought it

would be more polite. Some of the soldiers looked too young to be veterans; then I remembered the Gulf War. A group of vets with "Vietnam" on their jackets or caps stood to my right. *Fakers*, I thought, because they also looked too young to be veterans; then I felt bad again for my petty thoughts. Because what if I was wrong? I asked an old guy if I could see his program, and he offered to sign it for me. I felt bad later because it didn't hit me until hours afterward that he, too, must have been a veteran even though he wasn't wearing a uniform. At the time I only felt embarrassed and confused by his offer. I should have said yes. I should have said thank you.

After a moment of silence at eleven A.M., the 177th Air Fight Wing did a flyover. It was as if a bomb had gone off from one end of the sky to the other. (Later I read people's posts on Echo, wondering what the explosion was.) Veterans started laying wreaths by the flagpole. An announcer named the donor of each wreath. Someone standing too close to the microphone told the announcer to hurry up. He did. The veterans laying the wreaths had to run. *Why won't they let them take their time?* It was all over in thirty seconds. Then a veteran named Rick Carrier stepped up wearing a beautiful, well-preserved brown wool uniform and asked us to come forward and sing. I fell in love with his smile. I tried to picture what he must have looked like forty or so years ago. He must have fought in the Korean War because he didn't look older than sixty. Which branch has brown uniforms? I wondered.

Someone handed me a photocopied pamphlet entitled "101 Songs You Love to Sing." Almost everyone had left by this time. I stayed and sang with about a dozen elderly ladies and gentlemen, Rick, the cops on duty watching us, and the smokers across the street. We sang "America the Beautiful," "My Buddy," "Bye, Bye Blackbird," "Give My Regards to Broadway," "The Yankee Doodle Boy," and "You're a Grand Old Flag." I had to stop on "After the Ball." I had had enough singing. I went over to the wreaths. The man who had offered me his autograph was there. It still hadn't occurred to me that he was a vet, so I didn't say anything. We stood together silently and watched someone from the Parks Department disentangle the huge American flag from the tree it had got caught in when they lowered it to half-mast.

After the ball is over,
After the break of morn,
After the dancers' leaving,
After the stars are gone;
Many a heart is aching,
If you could read them all;
Many the hopes that have vanish'd,
After the ball.

fantasy

GEORGE BALANCHINE ONCE SAID, "Everything that man does he does for his ideal woman." When my answering machine stopped working recently and I traced the problem to the red wire inside the phone jack, I thought, *My ideal man will appreciate that I could do that. He'll love Brazilian music and be thrilled that I can play it, and he will agree that the sound system is the most important feature of a movie theater and be grateful that I know which theaters in Manhattan have the best.*

In my fantasies I am ideal for my ideal man and I have one particularly embarrassing but treasured fantasy that shows just how this works.

I'm giving a talk about cyberspace in a large auditorium in California that is filled with people from another online service called The WELL, who hate me. A number of people from The WELL do, in fact, hate me, for all sorts of reasons, real and imaginary, but in reality most people on The WELL have never even heard of me. In my fantasy, however, most of the people in the audience have heard of me and the only reason they're there is to give me a piece of their mind.

I start to speak but I am immediately interrupted by hostile questions. I notice an elderly man in the front row. He is in a wheelchair and hooked up to some sort of elaborate life-support system. He's gathering his things together to leave and he looks upset. A kind, gentle-looking man in his forties or fifties—perhaps his son—is helping him.

"What's wrong?" I ask the old man.

He looks at me and says, "I don't know who you are and why these people hate you. You seem like a nice girl to me. But I came here to see a performance of *Pirates of Penzance* and I must have gotten the night wrong. You see, I'm dying. And I have always had this fantasy." In my fantasies everyone has treasured fantasies. "I'm in the audience and a pretty young woman is about to sing 'Poor Wand'ring One.' She sees me and something clicks, we make a connection, and she turns and sings the entire song just to me, as if I'm the only person in the hall.

"When I heard that they were going to do *Pirates of Penzance* here tonight, I thought, *I'm dying, what have I got to lose? Maybe a miracle will happen. Life is so hard, and I don't have any time left for my fantasies to come true—what the hell, it's a stupid fantasy, maybe life will throw me a bone. You never know.*

"So I got here and I saw you, a pretty young thing"—to him I am a pretty young thing—"and I made the mistake of hoping that it just might happen. It's such a small thing. Maybe, just maybe, before I die one of my fantasies, for once, will come true.

"But of course it didn't. It's a stupid fantasy, I'm a stupid man, and I'm going to die."

He starts to cry. The younger man with him gives me an

apologetic look and reaches for their things to leave. I walk over to the old man's side of the stage, take off my glasses, look him straight in the eye, and start to sing.

> *Poor wand'ring one!*
> *Tho' thou hast surely strayed,*
> *Take heart of grace,*
> *Thy steps retrace,*
> *Poor wand'ring one!*
> *Poor wand'ring one!*
> *If such poor love as mine*
> *Can help thee find*
> *True peace of mind,*
> *Why, take it, it is thine!*

I stop, because those are all the words I know, and there has to be some possibility, however remote, that the things I imagine could technically happen, or the fantasy isn't satisfying. I am like the old man. Deep down I think there is some chance my fantasies might come true. So they have to be bound by reality. It improves my odds. I can't sing very well, but for the old man and me, that's not the point.

The man helping the old man is indeed his son. He is also, of course, my ideal man. I walk down, take the old man's hand, and kiss him. His son whispers, "Thank you," and grabs the flyer with my name on it because he will call me later and we will fall in love. They leave. I walk back up and try to continue my talk, but I cry instead because the old man is going to die and we're all going to die, but at least we had a moment of in-between glory. The hostility in the audience has disappeared— not because they don't hate me anymore (the reality constraint again) but because the old man is going to die and they're going to die and even though they hate me, they know a moment of in-between glory when they see it and they don't want to wreck it.

I know how sentimental this fantasy is, but I never get tired of it. I told it to my friend Marianne. "What happens to the people from The WELL who hate you?" she asked. "Can they burst into flames while you're singing or something?"

cats

Veets and Beams—A Personality Profile

veets

Friendly, outgoing, Veets likes people. He'll go up to anyone. I've decided he must have been treated decently before being dropped off at the Center for Animal Care and Control to be adopted or killed. I used to put Veets in a bag and take him riding with me on the back of my friend's motorcycle and he didn't mind.

Veets is smart. He can open the refrigerator and any drawer or cabinet in the apartment. When he gets into the fridge, he pokes a hole in the carton of half-and-half with one of his claws, then he laps it up as it pools on the floor. I had to install a hook and eye to keep the door closed, but sometimes I forget to use it. I say, "Bad cat," whenever he gets inside, but I don't mean it. I'm proud of his accomplishment.

Veets is afraid of change and I think he got this from me. I once took him to a park on Staten Island when I was feeling bad about the fact that he never got to play outside. I laid out a blanket and a book for myself, then put Veets on the grass. It was like putting the same poles of two magnets together. He popped right off the grass and back onto the blanket, shaking in fear. I picked him up and stuck him on a tree limb. He popped off the tree, too, then he popped off the grass again and landed back on the blanket. I gave up. Nature and Veets repel each other.

Veets always defers to Beams even though Veets was first. If Veets is curled up with me on the couch and Beamers jumps up, Veets will leave. I always say, "Don't let Beamers steal your spot," but I can't get him to come back. He will always give up the choice spots for Beams. Veets is a more satisfying cat to curl up with, too. Once Veets finds his spot, he'll stay there as long as you stay there—so long as Beamers isn't around.

Veets is calm, comforting, and solid. He's the first to meet me at the door when I come home at night.

beamers

Beamers never stays in one place for very long. He'll jump up on the couch and curl against me, then five minutes later he'll be on the chair. Then the floor. Then the bed. But he's softer than Veets. And more affectionate. Sometimes he pushes his head against mine and holds it there, breathing and purring into my neck. He purrs and nuzzles and treadles me whenever he's with me.

But only with me. Beamers is a scaredy-cat. Beamers hides when people come over. He must not have been treated well before being abandoned. He is more needy than Veets and demands more of my attention. He follows me wherever I go, has to be in the same room I'm in, has to sit on the papers I'm working on, has to sit on the book I'm reading, has to sit on my head when I'm lying on the couch watching TV. He's a pain in the ass, come to think of it. But—and I know I'm going to hell for this—Beamers is my favorite. He's my baby. I'm like a parent who doesn't want to admit she has a favorite, but I think it's because of his early health problems, and my having to feed him with an eyedropper for a week when I first took him home. We imprinted on each other.

I once read in a book that cats don't like you to stare at them but they do like it if you look at them and slowly blink. When I look at Beamers I slowly blink and he slowly blinks right back. Veets likes this, too, but Beamers will come up to me and initiate our blinking ritual, and no matter what I'm doing, I can't resist putting it aside to blink with Beams.

At thirteen and fourteen years old, respectively, Beams and Veets are at the start of their twilight years. They're slowing down. They used to do the Indy 500 up and down the hallway. They walk it now. Beamers, one year younger, can still jump up on the kitchen counter. Veets can't. They also used to go flying after Ping-Pong balls when I threw them. Now they don't even look up. They don't seem at all depressed about it, however. Beams still comes up for blinks, Veets still purrs when he gets uninterrupted time with me on the couch. They're as happy as ever. My cats are handling aging better than I am. My friend Joe, who also isn't thrilled to have hit forty, says the problem is that we're immature. We recognize ourselves in *Seinfeld* repeats and this pleases us. We never grew up, so we don't know how to grow old.

friendɟHip

JOE AND I KEEP WAITING for our friendship to turn into a *When Harry Met Sally* thing. We have this level of comfort with each other. When I was obsessing about my stomach, for instance, we compared fat rolls. Does it get any better than this? Feeling unself-conscious enough around someone to compare fat rolls? Joe and I can't help thinking things would be even better if we could somehow move into the more-than-friends category. We're so close. It's like watching the Wheel of Fortune tick, tick, ticking, through all the Friends slots while you hold your breath, hoping the ticking will stop on the Lovers slot. Jackpot. I've known Joe since 1987. We met when we were grad students.

Today on the phone Joe said, "Let's just get married." It wasn't the first time.

The problem is, we're not sexually attracted to each other.

We like each other more than almost anyone else, but we can't imagine kissing. If I can't imagine kissing a guy, well, I can't imagine marrying him. For reasons I don't understand, Joe doesn't think this is a problem.

"Joe, we have to solve the sex issue."

"Why?" he complains loudly. "Red says sex is not an issue. It's not about that, she says."

The Red he is referring to is our mutual friend Red Burns, the chair of the program where we were students and where I now teach. The basic argument goes something like this. After that initial intoxication, the importance of sex fades, and things like comparing fat rolls are what really keep you together and happy. Many people believe this. I once saw a documentary on PBS called *The Matchmaker*, and the matchmaker makes a similar point. Something that lasts only five or ten minutes (*Who is she having sex with?* I wondered) is not important.

Historically, marriage wasn't about either sex or love. It was about economics and politics. We changed the rationale to sex and love over time, as reasons of economics and politics became less compelling. Maybe the rationale will change again. In the future people may marry for friendship. Maybe Joe is simply ahead of his time. There is, I have to say, something exquisitely comforting about Joe's knowing when my TV holes are. TV holes are the times when there's nothing good on and it's safe to call. Is this enough to make a marriage?

Everyone else seems to think so. Red firmly believes that Joe and I will eventually wind up together. That we share only feelings of friendship seems to bother no one but me. *Look*, I want to tell them, *nothing would please me more. I hope my feelings for Joe change.* But Red and the matchmaker forget that while the act itself may be relatively brief, and the intensity of lust dims, being sexual with someone means more than engaging in sex. It changes the orientation of everything you do together. Every single thing. It's the romance. Walking with a friend is different from walking with your lover. Watching TV with a friend is different from watching TV with your lover. You don't have an "our song" with a friend. I don't know if one is better than the other.

I have an ongoing debate with my oldest friend, Chris. Which is better, single or married? Which are better, friends or lovers? Neither. Stalemate. They both have something going for them. And I want both. I couldn't bear life without romance. I know the common Stuart Smalley–like wisdom these days is that love doesn't save you, only you can save you, but I'm not looking to be saved. Nothing saves you. *I* can't fricking save me. But in the meantime, love is better than no love. A life without love is, bottom line, appalling and unacceptable. Period. Am I still leading a happy life? Yes. But I don't think my current state without romantic love is okay, not in any way, shape, or form.

The other night a friend who just became a father gave me a lift home. He very clearly wanted to kiss me. Without acknowledging what we were feeling, we stood next to his car on a block lush with ivy and wisteria, finding excuse after excuse to keep talking and stay close. The limbs of the gingko trees around us stretched up to the sky, grasping, as if longing for the stars. I hung in there, trying to come up with some reason that could possibly make it okay if we kissed. We kept turning to each other, thinking, *Maybe, maybe, maybe.* You think? *No.* Except? *No.* I gave up first, because, well, his son had just been born, but being enveloped in that kind of desire for a few minutes reminded me of not having it. All these women writing these I-don't-need-anybody-I'm-a-sassy-single-girl books can just go to hell.

I will concede that no love is better than love that isn't really working. That makes you feel worse. It's more lonely than being alone. In that case I'd just as soon be by myself or hang out with my friends. So I tell Joe we should be next-door neighbors instead. We could hang out together every day and sit around drinking coffee, gossiping about our friends, and comparing fat rolls. When I think about it, my friendships have been more enduring and contributed more to my overall happiness than my romances ever have. This seems to be true for all my friends as well. I'm not saying I don't want to find the man of my dreams. Who wants a life without love? But there has to be a reason why those we keep for life are friends more often than lovers.

"Marry me," Joe asks me again online. *Maybe I will, Joe. If I fall in love with you just a little bit more, maybe I will.*

work

WHEN IT COMES TO MONEY, it's sometimes hard to tell a dangerously insane person from someone who is basically okay. Perfectly normal people can become unhinged when faced with a billing problem. Take this guy, who had been on Echo for a couple of months and never paid us. The last invoice I sent him came back with this written across the front in pencil:

> *Go fuck yourself. I never joined your little club; therefore I owe you nothing. Your threats do not frighten me. If you do not back off, you will someday wish you had. (Believe it.) I do not expect to hear anything further from you or anyone else regarding this petty, absurd, annoying little matter. You are strongly advised to consider this, and decide if the consequences, whatever they turn out to be, are worth $64.35 to you. If you hand this off*

to someone else, it will not absolve you of the responsibility of starting a pissing match with me. Understand that when I take something personally, I can piss harder, and farther, and longer than any other man alive. And I never quit.

I am beginning to take this personally.

Very truly yours,
⟨name removed⟩
⟨phone number removed⟩

I'm sure you can piss harder, farther, and longer. That's because at least some of the other men alive have better things to do than pee really, really hard, crying out, "See? See?" That was my reaction. Then I thought, *How did I get here? To this job that makes me contend with people like this?* I looked into the guy's account. He hadn't used the service much, so I let the matter drop. I would lose in a confrontation with this kind of person. I would just stand there, frozen in shock that there were such people in the world and that their attention was directed at me. If he came at me with a gun, or a full bladder, I'd be a goner. The thing is, if I met Amazing Peeing Man at a cocktail party, I probably wouldn't suspect he was capable of writing such a note. It's the rare person who says, "Oh God, I'm sorry, I wasn't really using my account, I meant to close it." No. Not only do they owe you money, they have to be abusive about it on top of it. Then they have to come up with something to justify their hostility, like "Echo was so slow this month, and the phone lines kept disconnecting me." Anything to prove that you're the asshole, not them. But I've finally accepted that this is the defense that people adopt when they are in owing-money mode. This is how they cope.

Okay, I'm human. I'm not a saint. I still think a little less of them, and I'd like to think I'd behave better, but that's what everyone thinks.

My next career will *not* involve billing people. I'd rather die and seep onto my tie.

MUʃic

SHE SHOOTS, SHE SCORES. "Be at SOB's at one A.M. and wear all white," Ivo tells me at long last. Well, all-fucking-right. I've made it to the stage of SOB's. And it's like Christmas up here: lights everywhere, blinking, changing color. Everyone's shaking my hand, wishing me luck. The next forty minutes go by in a blur, but I do okay. No major drumming mistakes. Ivo's smiling at me for the first time I can remember. Unfortunately, my triumph lasts all of one set. Like everything else in life, that stage isn't all it's cracked up to be.

After Ivo announced that we'd be back in ten minutes, this guy comes up to me and looks me over.

HIM: Are you the girl that was drumming on the end?
ME: Yes. [I'm the only lefty in the band, and since I whack anyone who stands to my left, I always drum on the end.]

77

HIM: My friend wants to meet you, but he's too shy to come up to you himself. [He takes a closer look at me.] Are you sure you're the one who was on the end?
ME: Yes.
HIM: Take off your glasses.
ME: But I was wearing them while I was playing.
HIM: And you were definitely on the end?
ME: I was definitely on the end. *Get to the point!*

He looks around. "That's her!" He points to a girl who had been standing to my right. And there you have it, the famous invisibility that we all hear about. She's tall, cute as hell, barely twenty years old, and, as far as they're concerned, the one on the end.

And this is why I want to say "Fuck you" to that I'm-okay, I've-earned-my-wrinkles attitude that some people possess. Like I'm not supposed to have a problem with this? I try to cheer myself up. *Nothing lasts*, I say to myself. My standard line when bad things happen. Of course, that means nothing good will last, either. Except, when midlife life doesn't last, it's because you've entered the twilight years. When those don't last, you die.

cats

F OR YEARS THIS KEPT HAPPENING TO ME: I'd be walking along the street, listening to my Walkman, when someone in front of me would whip their head around and look at me with a startled and sometimes fearful or accusatory expression. When they saw me they'd relax, turn back around, and keep on walking. I thought I might be singing out loud without knowing it, except I am very self-conscious about my voice. Even on my most confident days I doubt I'd ever sing loud enough on the street for anyone to hear me. Besides, bad singing would not explain the looks people were giving me. I couldn't figure it out. By the time anyone turned to face me, any noise I might have been making would have been over, my mouth closed. And I was always too embarrassed to ask them what the problem was. It continued to be a mystery until the day my Walkman broke.

I was on the street, without music for the first time, when, out of the blue, I yelled—and I mean really yelled— "MUNCHES!" Short for "Munchkin," it's one of my many nicknames for Veets and Beams. A woman in front of me whirled around. I said, "Excuse me," and then tried to think what else I might have been screaming out all these years. Innocent terms of endearment that are sappy and sweet when said in the presence of an actual cat become downright psycho when yelled out by a woman out by herself wearing a Walkman. I can't imagine what the woman walking ahead of me thought "Munches" might mean. What else had I been yelling? The rest of that day I called out the following names:

"Belly." (This is one of Beamer's names. He has a big belly.)

"Poo." (Short for "Putter-Poo.")

"Baby-Cat" or "Baby-Boys" or sometimes just "Boy." (Or, worse still, the combination "Belly-Boys.")

"Boo." (It comes from "Boo-Cat," or "Baby-Boo.")

So it hit me: I am one of those crazy people who talks to herself on the street, one of the ones who makes you wonder where she came from and how she got to this sorry state. Great. How *did* I get to this sorry state, yelling to cats who are not there? The second I think of them I call out. Whatever internal lunatic-monitor most people possess is missing in me. Nothing represses this urge. I love my cats. I call out their names. They're so much a part of my life that it's a very short step from thinking of them to talking to them.

I might as well face it. I love my cats too much. You'll never see my neighbors standing around outside my apartment building with microphones in their faces, telling a local news reporter, "And she *seemed* so *normal*."

SUSANNE ROSEN

BORN ON NOVEMBER 12, 1923, in Brooklyn, New York, Sue is the mother of my friend Joe, the one who wants to marry me. That's because, I've now decided, he sees how well I take care of my cats. He's thinking of his twilight years.

Sue Rosen's drawings and watercolors got her into the prestigious High School of Music and Art. But it was way uptown and she was afraid to get on the subway, so she didn't go. She stopped painting when she went to college, where she studied education. She stopped working as a substitute teacher when she got pregnant.

She met her husband, Max, during Christmas week at Grossinger's Hotel in the Catskills. She was twenty-five and he was thirty-four. He was sitting on the couch reading *The New York Times*, and Sue asked if she could borrow his paper when he was done. He said okay, but added that she had to return it when she was finished, and she replied okay, I'll leave it for you here, under the pillow. He thought it was cute how she didn't know he was kidding. "I'm going to marry her," he told his friends. Two months later he proposed, on Valentine's Day, and they were married the following June. Their two children, Leah and Joe, are named after Max's parents. Joe is a computer programmer and Leah followed in her mother's footsteps—she got a teaching degree but stopped teaching when her children were young.

Sue Rosen never left Brooklyn. She had always meant to go to Europe but never did. Max, whom she calls Mac, died last year. Sue worked for two days straight cleaning out his closet. It's still full. "He didn't throw anything out."

Although I've been friends with Joe for more than ten years and Sue lives maybe an hour's ride away on the D train, we've never met. Joe kept calling me during my interview with his mother. When I didn't pick up the phone, he tried to reach me through e-mail and chat on the computer.

Are you old?

I'm beginning to feel old. When the bus stops for me they put the kneeling part down. I don't think I look old, but Joe says I look confused. He says people are nice to me because I look confused. I have half-Alzheimer's. I'm slowing down. I tire more easily. I talk about death all the time now. I'm preparing.

I immediately feel as comfortable with her as I do with Joe.

What are the main differences between the young you and the you now?

I used to get up feeling good. But now I feel like I don't have much to look forward to. When I was young I always felt like there was something more, there was always more ahead. I don't feel like that anymore. I don't feel like I have any more chances.

I start to feel uneasy.

Did you have a midlife crisis?

No. I was too busy. My whole life was what I have to do for my family and others. It became difficult when I didn't have to do anything for someone else. I always wanted to go to museums, but now that I can, I don't go.

I haven't had affairs, but I've thought about it.

How do you feel when you see your body in the mirror?

I used to like it. My husband always said I had a nice figure. But lately I'm shrinking. My body doesn't look as good to me. I used to be able to look down and see my figure nicely. Now, instead of being straight and nice, I look down and see a dent. It's just been this last year or two. I'd like to look better.

I don't know what she means by a dent and it doesn't get any clearer when she tries to explain it to me. I wonder if she imagines the dent the way my friends insist that I imagine I have a stomach.

What scares you?

I don't like to have anyone in my house. I don't like people to come here and clean for me. You see people who are sick and who have aides who come in to do everything for them. I don't ever want that. I'm afraid of being sick and dependent or going into a hospital and not being able to take care of myself.

And I don't want extraordinary measures taken to keep me alive.

Is there anything that no longer frightens you?

I'm more aggressive. I used to be very timid, but I think I got more aggressive because of my husband. I'd watch him.

Is there anything you no longer care about?

I don't want to paint anymore. I have no desire. It scares you, the thought that you are getting older. I just want to feel good so I can do whatever I feel like doing. I watch a lot of TV and I think that's terrible.

"I watch a lot of TV," I tell her. And then I think about all the things I don't do anymore either.

You are addressing someone you care about, someone young. Please finish this sentence. "If you only knew . . ."

No matter what you say, it doesn't mean anything to them. People have to experience it for themselves. I could say, "Cherish every day," but it won't matter. There's a time when you're young and you have the whole world in front of you and everyone dreams that they're going to grow up to be someone special. We all have those dreams. Then you have a few disappointments. You realize not everyone achieves those dreams. You wake up one morning and you realize, *This is it. I'm not going anywhere. I'm where I'm going to be.* That is when you really grow up.

Oh God.

Fast-forward to your deathbed. You're saying good-bye to friends and loved ones. Is there anything you've left unsaid that you'd like to say while you still have the chance?

Joe is not the kind of person to be sentimental. I would tell him how much I love him and there's nothing he could do that would ever make me feel differently. I never tell him. Whenever he leaves me after visiting, he won't let me go down to the car and say good-bye. I'd like to.

Which of your possessions would you hope will not be thrown out?

My photo albums. My high school yearbook, pictures of me from when I was young, pictures of my parents, letters that my father wrote my mother during the war, beautiful letters, my mother's report card, my father's passport from when he came to this country in 1912, and my father's and my husband's army discharge papers.

What would you like to experience one last time?

A great big family get-together. When my husband was dying we all knew it but we couldn't talk about it. We couldn't talk about anything personal. I could talk about the mail, or the children, but I couldn't talk about how I felt. I want to tell my children and my grandchildren how I feel. I do with my sister and my daughter but not with Joe and not with Mac. The few times Mac cried, it was very upsetting. I had a child who died when she was born, Michelle. Mac cried when he came to tell me. But usually when he got upset he'd get quiet. Whenever any of us got sick, he'd get upset and be quiet.

Looking back on it all, what will you miss the most?

Food, chocolate ice cream, nice hot showers, reading. I used to read the classics but now I prefer light reading, romantic books. I like romantic movies. I like walking on Avenue M. Everything I need is on Avenue M: the beauty parlor, the drugstore, Pick & Pay Butcher, Amazing Savings Housewares—it has books, clothing, it's a general store.

Whom will you miss the most?

Right now I miss Mac. I miss seeing him across the table. I miss going to a restaurant and having him there with me. It's always the worst at dinnertime. After Mac, my children and my grandchildren.

Was it worth it? Why?

Sometimes tomorrow never came. The things I hoped would come, didn't. I thought there was more romance in life than I found to be there. I would have liked a more exciting love affair.

Oh God, oh God, oh God.

deatH

SUE REMINDED ME what I was afraid of. Some of us get to the end and realize that time's up, that the things we wanted more than anything are never going to happen. I can't stop thinking about this. When we were kids we all thought it would go differently. I look at people on the subway platform. All these people. They all long for the same kinds of things I do. "Everyone dreams that they're going to grow up to be someone special," Sue had said. Rock stars, movie stars, Nobel Prize winners, whatever. I don't know whether everyone has the same kinds of grandiose dreams that I do, but I can tell you that few of us are going to succeed. Millions of people. A few hundred rock stars. It gets worse. Sometimes the most horrible thing you can imagine happens. Somebody's got to be the one to get on an airplane, a little scared that it will crash, and then when the nose actually does pitch down, scream, "Oh my God, it's really happening this time! No no no no no!"

Diane Keaton recently came out with a book of old newspaper photographs from the forties and fifties; picture of battered wives, families of lost children, convicted killers and the bodies of their victims. "These were people who didn't know who they were and they weren't going to have the chance to find out," she wrote.

The most horrible thing you can imagine doesn't have to be so dramatic. The little nightmares really get you. Joe told me that he hadn't known his mother had ever given her stillborn child a name. Then he told me something he knew I'd really like to know. Michelle Rosen is buried on Hart Island, which sits out in the Long Island Sound between the Bronx and Long Island. Hart Island is New York's potter's field. The term "potter's field" comes from the Gospel of St. Matthew. Judas, miserable about his betrayal of Jesus, couldn't wait to get rid of the thirty pieces of silver he'd been paid, so he threw them into the Temple. The priests didn't want to put blood money into the treasury. After talking it over, they used the money to buy land from a local potter to use as a cemetery for strangers. Potter's fields are traditionally where the poor, unclaimed, and unidentified are buried. Hart Island has been Sue Rosen's little nightmare for forty-two years.

Joe was eager to tell me about Michelle because he knew about my fascination with cemeteries. He also knew that I'd been trying to get to Hart Island for years. It's the final resting place of New York's most forgotten. If I can remember the dead on Hart Island, then I've won. The closest I ever got to Hart Island was when a friend took me to the west side by boat. We couldn't land. A big sign on the beach reads, "Prison. Keep Off." Hart Island is maintained by the New York City Department of Corrections and it's almost impossible to get permission to visit. What reason could I give them?

When Joe told me that his sister was there, I had just learned that finally, after all these years, I was going to be able to step off that boat and onto the rocks and mussel shells that cover the beaches of Hart Island. I was at work when I was invited to join someone going out to the island in a couple of weeks and I couldn't work anymore: instant daydreaming. There would be strong winds, I knew, and the smell of the Long Island Sound had to be the same as on the Huntington side. Would I hear leaves blowing? Are there enough leaves to make any noise on Hart Island? "Do you think your mother's going to be okay about me knowing she's there?" I asked Joe, referring to Michelle. "Sure. Call her. The Widow's tough." Joe calls his mother the Widow. But I didn't call her immediately. What could I say? "How do you feel about the fact that your baby is buried in potter's field?" I'd go there first, I decided, and then call to tell her. I was convinced that Hart Island was going to turn out to be a lovely little dream, a better place than any cemetery or mausoleum, and I didn't want to talk to her before I could tell her that with authority.

MY work to-do List

- Change the backup tape for Echo.
- Pay phone bill.
- Answer e-mail.

I'M 421 MESSAGES BEHIND, so this last item is high on the list. Instead, I log in to Echo and go to the Secret Space. The Secret Space is a private place on Echo where I talk to a dozen friends, obsessively, all day long. At the moment, everyone is talking about food. Specifically, they are wondering whether raisins are evil and why would anyone put them in bagels.

Then I answer a hundred e-mail messages, getting to the people whose letters begin "Why haven't you answered my e-mail yet?" first. After that I log in to the Secret Space to see what I've missed while answering e-mail. They are describing the home of their dreams.

- Ask Angus to fix the billing program bugs.
- Write three new cat pieces and fax them to Betsy.

Betsy is my agent. I write one cat piece, and then I log back in to the Secret Space to upload another piece I'm working on to find out whether people think it's too depressing. They don't.

- Call the people with invalid credit card numbers and get the right numbers.
- Call veterinarian about the noises Beamers made last night.
- Call Joe and Chris. Should I cut my hair short?
- Ask Jenn to update our equipment list.
- Call Mom.

I return my mother's phone call from a week earlier. I ask her how everyone is—my brothers, Douglas and Peter, and their families; my stepsister, Janet, and her kids. They're all fine. I'm fine, too, I tell her. She tells me she's fine. Then I call my stepmother and learn that she and my father are fine as well.

- Play voice mail.

Seven people are having problems with their modems. Twenty people have billing questions. Betsy likes the new piece from last week. Chris wants to know if I'll come out to Long Island to visit her. Back in the Secret Space they're deciding which *Buffy the Vampire Slayer* character they would rather go to bed with, Spike or Angel. "Spike," I say.

- Mail invoices to people whose credit cards were declined.

- Send e-mail to people whose accounts will be closed for nonpayment.
- Put together speaker schedule for the class I teach at New York University.

I teach "Virtual Culture," a course about online society. I spend an hour picking guest speakers, then I send e-mails to invite them. Meanwhile, a fight about home schooling has broken out in the Secret Space. Two people who work in the New York City public school system are pointing out the flaws of home schooling. "Where else will children be socialized?" one asks. More than one person responds, "We all went to school and, well, look at us."

- Send bank statements to accountant.
- Buy cat litter, socks, printer labels, stamps, lightbulbs, and the Café Tacuba CD.
- Ask Bob Knuts if he'll call my landlord.

My landlord scares me.

- Look at WellEngaged.

The software that runs Echo is obsolete. I've been talking for years about replacing it but haven't found anything I like yet. There's a program called WellEngaged, written by the people at The WELL, the online service I copied when I created Echo, but as of this writing I still haven't found what I need. It will be the death of us.

- Fax press release about "Live Chat with Writer Joe Connelly" to media contacts.
- Ask at staff meeting: What should we do about the scary entomologist?

There's a guy on Echo who suffers from blackouts. He's aware of the problem, but he won't acknowledge it when it happens. For example, he'll log in at night, write a bunch of stuff, and then log in the next morning and ask, "Who wrote all that?" We're not sure what to do.

- Pick up stuff at the copy shop.
- Send thank-you note to Allison for the Phil Ochs album.

I was talking on Echo about looking for the Phil Ochs album *Pleasures of the Harbor,* and a few days later Allison sent me her copy of it. Just like that. The album. Not a tape of the album, the album itself.

I check into the Secret Space. Now they're arguing about evolution and giving career advice to one of our younger members.

- Return Company A and Company B's phone calls.

Two companies have just approached me about buying Echo. I want to sell it—believe me, I can't sell it fast enough. I've got that TV life I want to live, and bills are getting harder and harder to pay. Still, I can't imagine life without Echo. It would be like death on training wheels for me. I know that someday I'll be in a nursing home, barely able to move, staring out a closed window in an overheated room, and describing these days of twenty-four-hour-a-day camaraderie as my golden days. But everyone so far who has approached me about buying Echo has huge Internet dollar signs in their eyes, and I know they are seeing America Online rather than my beloved dysfunctional family, Echo. Besides, what would become of our Secret Space?

Except I know people at both companies, one of them well.

- Call Mauro. Going to New Jersey gig?
- Call Ivo about the New Jersey gig. Time?

I go to the Secret Space and ask, Should I bother to buy a new shirt for the New Jersey gig? Because maybe the man of my dreams will be there.

I think for a minute, then add one more line to my list:

- Get materials about Echo ready to show Company A and Company B.

romance

I'VE GOT SIX DAYS LEFT to find redemption by Christmas and it's not looking good. So far I'm just doing what has always failed in the past. First I go to *The Nutcracker*. When, oh when, will I ever remember how boring it is? The whole first act, with all those children who can't dance yet, and the Christmas tree growing right there on the stage, which is not exciting and never was, even when I was seven, although I pretended it was for the sake of my grandmother, who seemed eager for me to be thrilled by it all. She must have been looking for her redemption through me. I'll bet it's people like us who keep the New York State Theater box office busy every winter: people who will never learn, who keep going back, some dragging their children and grandchildren, creating an endless stream of audiences whose disappointment will drift over the seats and onto the stage, giving the ballet a depth it wouldn't have if not for our failed hope. An evil tradition.

Next I went to the *Messiah* sing-along at St. Luke's Church. Mistake. I was surrounded by a bunch of tuneless, determined sopranos. Not that I'm such a great singer, because I'm not at all, but at least I know when to sing quietly. I tried to be a better person. I smiled at all the awful sopranos around me as if I didn't care how annoyingly bad they were, but then they fake-smiled back at me and my fake generosity went right out the window. *Can't you hear yourselves?* I thought, in a snit. *You can't sing for shit, and you're not singing for shit nonstop forte, you redemption-wreckers.*

The problem isn't *The Nutcracker*, or *The Messiah*, or even Christmas. It's *War and Peace*. Winter makes me think of *War and Peace* and a troika ride in the snow around the middle of the novel. That ride lays out exactly how I will sabotage any chance I have of ever finding the man of my dreams. It was while reading Tolstoy that I first realized this was actually a possibility, that you could reach a point when you are alone for the rest of your life. One night you could sleep with someone, and that person could be the last person you will sleep with for the rest of your life. After that, not even my old standby, denial, which keeps me safe the rest of the year, could get me through Christmas. Tolstoy completely nails me with the character Sonya, who doesn't even get a last name, as far as I can tell. She starts out young and alive, her Victorian bosom heaving with hope and love for her cousin Nicholas, the man of her dreams, who promises to marry her. At a dinner party she is filled with such excitement she can't focus on anyone else for more than a few seconds. When Nicholas flirts with the lovely heiress Julie Karagina, not even noticing that Sonya is sitting there, watching the whole thing, she flees, unable to hold her desperate, forced smile. Nicholas leaves for the army shortly after. Remember this part.

On Nicholas's first leave home from the army, his sister, Natasha, tells him of Sonya's words of devotion and sacrifice, spoken when Sonya was carried away, as only a young girl in love for the first time can be. " 'I shall love him always, but let him be free.' Isn't that lovely and noble?" Natasha asks her brother, quoting Sonya. Nicholas says he won't go back on his word—the right response. Then Natasha explains that no, he's got it all wrong; this is exactly what she and Sonya thought he would say, but "if you consider yourself bound by your promise—it will seem as if she had not meant it seriously. It makes it as if you were marrying her because you must, and that wouldn't do at all." Sweet, stupid children.

Natasha is the one who has it all wrong. I know exactly what Sonya was thinking. It isn't that she didn't mean what she said in all her glorious innocence, but she wasn't making a sacrifice without longing. Deep down, she hoped her nobility would be rewarded. She was proving her love. He was supposed to prove his by insisting. He was supposed to say that he wasn't marrying her because he had to, he was marrying her because he wanted to. But Nicholas takes Sonya at her (or his sister's) word. He goes back to the army, leaving open the possibility that he may one day marry Sonya. And of course she hopes. How can she not?

But Sonya has let Nicolas off the hook. I'm not sure what she should have done next. I just know in my heart that she set herself up. To look at this simply as Nicholas stringing the innocent Sonya along would be a mistake. Something important would be missed—Sonya's fatal misstep—and it's imperative that I find it because the minute I started reading about Sonya, I started coming up with reasons why my life is really nothing like hers, really it isn't, I swear, because I have all these reasons here, see. But I know now that I am on the exact same path, doing the exact same thing, and that if I don't figure it out, I'm going to end up just like her. And she doesn't end up well.

I haven't been able to put my finger on it yet. It's even harder now because one of my cats—I'm pretty sure it was Veets, the older, fatter one, and the one with dandruff no matter what I do—did that kneading thing cats do on my copy of *War and Peace*, and it's so old the pages have crumbled to pieces, whole chapters at a time. Veets and Beams hate me to cut their nails, so I don't. (An indication of the kind of parent I would be.) I'm convinced the answers are in the missing pages. But do I go out and get another copy to save my romantic life? Of course not.

I've figured out Sonya's first mistake. She gets so caught up in this image of herself as a tragic heroine that she misses how easily Nicholas accepts her fantasy. "I am lovely and noble and you should be free!" And he thought, *Okay.* Had he loved her he would have been in agony, thinking that perhaps she was suggesting that he be free because she was really the one who wanted to be released. She should have picked up on this. But no, she doesn't see that while she has the fantasy of being the noble orphan (she was a ward in their home), he does not have the companion fantasy of seeing himself as her rescuer. Their fantasies didn't complement each other. He wants her to be a tragic heroine. Everyone in the family does. They are in financial trouble and he has to rescue all of them. No one wants him to marry the penniless orphan.

Tolstoy tortures her (me) throughout. By the time of that passage describing how they're all dressed up in costumes for the troika ride, Nicholas still hasn't declared himself. Sonya's costume is the best of all. She puts on a fake mustache and eyebrows, and everything changes. They all go on and on about how handsome she looks, and their attention releases her. Sonya's more animated than she's ever been. She knows it is now or never, and she makes the most of it. Nicholas notices the change at once. When he turns to look at her in her sable furs, he sees a newly radiant Sonya in the moonlight and he simply can't take his eyes off her.

> "So that is what she is like; what a fool I have been!" he thought gazing at her sparkling eyes, and under the mustache a happy rapturous smile dimpled her cheeks, a smile he had never seen before.
> "I'm not afraid of anything," said Sonya.

Well, she should have been. Nicholas never looks at her like that again. He never marries her and she never finds the man of her dreams. He marries Princess Mary, and Sonya moves in with them and their children and endures a life without love. Tolstoy tries to make this turn of events okay by making Princess Mary plain and unattractive but a good soul. He surrounds her with men who want to marry her for her money, so when Nicholas marries her for love it's almost a good thing. Also, by marrying an heiress, he is saving his family. But what Tolstoy does to Sonya is unforgivable. With the dispassion of scientists discussing an insect they've dissected, Nastasha and Princess Mary, both of whom are living with the men of *their* dreams, talk about Sonya's loveless lot. Natasha calls her a "sterile flower." Like certain varieties of strawberry blossoms, she says. Then Tolstoy goes in for the kill:

> "Sometimes I am sorry for her and sometimes I think she doesn't feel it as you or I would. . . ."
> It really seemed that Sonya did not feel her position trying, and had grown quite reconciled to her lot as a sterile flower. She seemed to be fond not so much of individuals as of the family as a whole. Like a cat, she attached herself not to people but to the home. She waited on the old countess, petted and spoiled the chil-

dren, was always ready to render the small services for which she had a gift, and all this was unconsciously accepted from her with insufficient gratitude.

Not only do they screw her in the end, they're saying that only they, not Sonya, fully comprehend and feel her tragedy. Fuck them all and Tolstoy, too. Sonya feels. For over a thousand pages she feels. But they have to say that she doesn't, because to believe otherwise would be unbearable. To have the girl whose face was once lit with a "rapturous smile" when she thought she was on the verge of finally realizing her dreams live on, fully conscious of her loveless fate, mistreated, in the house of the man who once couldn't leave her side? No. Tolstoy ties up that loose end (me!) with, "Oh, she's okay with being a sterile flower." I hate them all.

How many Christmases do I have left to figure out how to avoid Sonya's fate? She fancied herself a noble victim, and life granted her wish. If I don't figure it out, life will fulfill my wrapped-up-in-death-and-alone-with-cats fantasy. Everything was in front of Sonya when she was sixteen; it must all still be in front of me, too. Any number of moments could have been the now-or-never moment of my life. *What am I missing?*

So every Christmas I try to find something that will save me. *The Nutcracker* and *The Messiah* aren't it. The holiday party at Echo had a couple of good moments, but they sputtered out from lack of momentum. I thought I might buy Veets and Beams some gifts, but they're cats and they don't know the difference. I'd just be a vampire redeemer like my grandmother.

I watched *It's a Wonderful Life*, the *Buffy* Christmas episode, and every other special I could. I've been listening to all the cassettes I've been collecting over the years: *Anne Murray's Christmas, Harry Connick Jr.'s Christmas, Mario Lanzo's Christmas*—I played the Snoopy Christmas song six times. I should probably give up on this whole Christmas-will-save-me thing, but I know I won't. Oh no. I just had a Sonya moment. I think Sonya's problem was that she either wouldn't or couldn't recognize that she never had a chance with Nicholas and therefore wasted her whole life waiting. She should have cut her losses and moved on. I'm dooming myself by refusing to let go of my own hopeless fantasies. If I don't let go of the fantasy, I won't get anything real.

Give up on Christmas, give up on Christmas. And embrace what? I thought of volunteering at the Veterans' Hospital. After the poorly attended parade last Memorial Day, someone got up and said, "If you appreciate the vets, please visit them on the holidays." I already knew, as I thought, *Yes!*, all carried away, that I wouldn't.

Pretty soon I'm going to go out and try to find my mother a Christmas present. She's the only one I'm buying a present for this year. While I'm out I'm taping *Miracle on 34th Street.* My mother won't be happy with whatever I buy her, and *Miracle on 34th Street* won't save me. *Give up on Christmas, give up on Christmas.* Except I can't. I can't pretend that I've relinquished my redemption fantasy any more than I can fake tolerance for lousy sopranos.

Please make it not too late for me, Spirits of Christmases to come. I'm a real person and not a character in a novel. I don't want to be a sterile flower. I know that Tolstoy is wrong. I know I will feel it and I know it will hurt.

cats

Cats experience longing, and I have proof. About ten years ago a mouse ran across my kitchen floor and disappeared beneath the stove. Veets, who was just a few feet away, went crashing into the stove after him, but he wasn't fast enough. The mouse got away. For the rest of the night Veets waited by the stove. I woke up at three in the morning to go to the bathroom and he was still sitting there, waiting. We never saw the mouse again.

Ten years later, Veets still waits. Every few nights, year after year, he goes over to the stove and sits and stares at the exact spot where he hit his head going after the mouse. Someday, he's sure, that mouse will return. He won't give up. He looks like the RCA dog.

It breaks my heart. I almost want to buy him a mouse to reward his undying kitty faith, but I've seen what cats do to mice when they catch them. I know what the crunch of tiny bones sounds like. And that half-growl, half-meow of perfect satisfaction they make is just a little too primal for me.

Once, I told him the truth. "That mouse is never coming back," I told him. But he didn't believe me. Veets will keep hoping until the day he dies. Me too, Veets. The man of my dreams is out there. But sometimes I worry that Veets and I will end up covered in cobwebs and disappointment, waiting, Miss Havisham–like, forever.

fAMiLy

IT WAS HELL trying to get my mother to tell me where my grandmother Daisy was buried. First she couldn't remember the name of the hospital where Daisy died. "It was in Glendale, in Queens." It turned out to be a hospital in Brentwood, on Long Island. Then she couldn't remember where Daisy was buried, although in this case what she told me was closer to the truth: "It was something Immaculate Conception in Queens." No Immaculate Conceptions. "Look for a cemetery on Metropolitan Avenue." I found Daisy in St. John's Cemetery on Metropolitan Avenue in Middle Village, a small, old-fashioned-looking neighborhood in Queens that I'll bet hasn't changed much since my grandmother was buried there in 1951. I couldn't find anywhere to eat breakfast when I went out there. It was just one huge cemetery after another as I walked down Metropolitan Avenue to St. John's. *I gotta move here.*

Daisy Armstrong lies in section 15, range B, plot 21, grave 3. There are a lot of dead people in New York. There are seventeen people in my grandmother's grave alone. They range in age from a stillborn with no name who was buried in 1941, to the oldest, the stillborn's mother, Helen Craven, who died when she was seventy-nine. The burials started with James Craven in 1928—he was only seven months old—and they ended in 1991 with Kelly R. Coder, who only lived a week. How many other graves are packed like this? You wouldn't know that all those people were in there by looking at the gravestone. Only two people are listed: Thomas F. Craven, who died in 1938 at age seventy-one, and his wife, Rose Anna Craven, who died in 1929 at age sixty.

You also wouldn't know all those people are in there by the width of the plot; it's as narrow as every other grave. I can't help wondering how they do this. It must be a matter of depth. Did they know when they buried Jimmy Craven that they'd be burying sixteen people on top of him, and bury him very, very deep? Or do they take people out and dig deeper? That would get kind of messy, wouldn't it? Because some time had passed and there had to be a certain amount of decay, were they able to, well, smush everyone down?

The great-grandfather I look like, Claude Corke, whose picture hangs on the wall next to me, is in there along with his wife, the former Jennie Lynch. I'm trying to track down Jennie's father, James Lynch, who fought in the Civil War. I couldn't believe it when I learned there was a forgotten veteran in my own family. He won't be forgotten for long. I'll find you, James Lynch. What is this thing I have with veterans? But James Lynch is not one of the seventeen people buried in my family's mass grave.

The grave is marked by a medium-sized cross. I wish I knew Latin. At the top of the cross are the letters IHS. That's got to be Latin, and not an acronym for "I Hate Stacy," which was my first guess. There's also a burning heart above Thomas and Rose Anna's names, which means I don't know what. Some overwrought Catholic burning-heart-of-someone thing.

It's dark and green and quiet in St. John's Cemetery. I could curl up in the grass, my head against the stone, and dream of all the people, of all the lives piled up beneath the earth. Acres of land and trees and marble angels, lambs and burning hearts, but I didn't see another soul while I recited the only two prayers I could remember (and I couldn't remember them exactly): the Lord's Prayer and the Hail Mary, which I sang in Latin (Schubert's "Ave Maria"). My heart beat fast as I knelt on top of the grave and sang. It was something to be above the resting spot of Claude and Daisy. It was almost thrilling. They're the ones I pray to all the time. Their pictures are right next to me now. And it took me forty-two years to get here. It was like being on a treasure hunt, and their remains were the prize.

ƒANTAƒY

I USED TO FANTASIZE about saving the life of John F. Kennedy, Jr., who in my daydreams was always being held at gunpoint by some trembling, frightened lunatic. I don't know what the lunatic wanted; it wasn't important to my fantasy. What was important was that I was a hero because I wouldn't let another Kennedy get shot. And I get to say, "No, no, please, don't, please," all embarrassed, when Jackie tries to thank me. (I changed it to Ted after Jackie died.)

It's too late now, of course, but during that week before we learned he was unsavable forever, I figured out how I might have rescued him from that crashing plane. All the experts were weighing in on what went wrong, and for a while the consensus was that his plane went into a "graveyard spiral." So I went onto Echo and asked what a graveyard spiral was, exactly, and how does one recover from it? As I've said, my fantasies don't work unless they are, at least to some extent, plausible. I can't rescue Kennedy if I don't honestly know how to get out of a graveyard spiral. I had to learn. I also needed to know because rescuing myself and others from plummeting planes remains another one of my most cherished fantasies. This information will be useful on an ongoing-fantasy basis. I'll be prepared when the pilot of my plane suffers a heart attack, and I have just fallen forward out of my seat because of our downward tilt, and, because I didn't have my seat belt on, I've landed right next to the pilot, who I notice—oh my God!—has died and—updated version—we're in a graveyard spiral!

But I don't understand the instructions. They say the first thing to do is "roll the wings level." Level to what? Is this something you would see on your instrument panel? On Echo, even the pilots can't agree. No, you don't bring the wings level. The first thing you should do is let go of the controls altogether and allow the plane to fall. It will right itself. Then you pull up slowly. But the guys on TV say that pulling up will only make the spiral tighter. "Oh, you're asking about a spiral?" they reply. "We were talking about a *spin*." If I were on a plummeting plane with a bunch of people from Echo, we'd be reviewing our options all the way to the bottom of the deep blue sea. But this is even better. Now I have instructions for getting out of either a spin or a spiral, except I can't really keep the difference straight in my mind, and what's more important as far as the Kennedy rescue fantasy is concerned, how am I supposed to tell in time to do anything about it? His plane was supposedly at two thousand feet when it started falling. The radar indicated that it fell roughly a thousand feet in fourteen seconds. When is it too late to recover?

I spend a minute imagining what happens to the people inside a small plane locked in a graveyard spiral, dropping a thousand feet in fourteen seconds. They'd be bounced violently back and forth in a circular motion that might or might

not feel like a circle; it might just be this unknowable, uniden-
tifiable motion. And all this in utter darkness with no idea if
this motion—spin? spiral?—is taking them up or down. I decide that, okay, maybe an expert would never have gotten into
this mess in the first place, but even for an expert, getting out
of it would be some piece of work. To focus on the instruments
to correctly assess which mess you're in—spin? spiral?—and
then take the appropriate action before it's too late?

I decide the only plausible scenario for my fantasy would
be one in which I panic. "Wait!" I shout at Kennedy. This is
something I would do. "Just give me a second to think here!"
Kennedy is in a panic, too, so he freezes, which turns out to
be exactly the right thing to do. Computer geeks have a saying:
"That's not a bug, that's a feature." They like to convince you
that something that appears bad is actually good if you just look
at it the right way. In my fantasy I turn a bug—panic—into a
feature. Because whether you're in a spin or a spiral, your first
impulse, to pull up, will kill you. Better to panic. Reality requirement satisfied.

Explanation of how I was in the plane in the first place: I
am at the airport, looking at planes and dreaming about rescuing someone, when John and Carolyn and Lauren walk by
with a mutual friend (we do have mutual friends) who waves
to me and asks, "Have you gotten over your fear of flying yet?"
And I say, "No, but I'd love to get on a small plane and give
it a try"—which is true: I'm afraid of flying but my main fear
is of jets, not single-engine Piper Saratogas—and Kennedy
looks back at me over his shoulder, smiles his beautiful, perfect
smile that I will never see again, except in my fantasies, and
says cheerfully, "Hop in."

The next thing I do in my Kennedy-rescue fantasy is, if
we're in a spiral, look at the attitude indicator and level my
wings (note to self: have someone show me an attitude indicator and tell me how to read it, otherwise I can't continue to

savor this fantasy—reality proportions off) or, if we're in a spin, let the plane continue to fall until it regains some lift and then, in both cases, slowly pull back up.

The fantasy ends with everyone returning to their families. Rory's wedding takes place, John is embarrassed but gracious about all the coverage, and I go back to New York alone because the Kennedys and I are not really friends and that's not what this fantasy is about. I've never forgotten watching my mother cry when his father died. I don't want to be a part of that world, I just want to keep it in place.

deАtH

IF I DIE IN BAY SHORE, and if he's still around and in the funeral business—because I plan to live until at least 2050—I want Anthony Scotti to take care of all the arrangements. Scotti is the director of the Bay Shore Funeral Home, and I went to see him after falling asleep immediately following a teaser for a news piece on television about unclaimed ashes left in funeral homes. Boxes of people stacked and abandoned. Such an awful package to be left behind, forgotten. I read an article years ago about a baby's coffin found in a toolshed at the New York City Marble Cemetery. The child's parents had fled Cuba in the 1960s. They wanted to bury their baby back home, after Castro's fall, so they paid a caretaker to look after the coffin until that time. But that time never came and they never returned for their infant.

The next morning I called the TV station that ran the

unclaimed-ashes story and they directed me to Anthony Scotti. I was expecting someone like Angus Scrimm's Tall Man character from the *Phantasm* movies, and instead I got this wonderful Long Island boy with a sweet laugh, who got into the funeral business because there had been no line for the mortuary sciences guy on Career Day at the H. Frank Carey High School. Anthony told me he'd rather die than go into a nursing home, and that if he had it to do all over again, he'd go into forensic science.

When Anthony bought the Bay Shore Funeral Home in 1994, he added a couple of dozen boxes of ashes to a growing collection kept in a storage room in the chapel at Oakwood Cemetery. They've got ashes going back to the 1940s, when the boxes were still made of metal. (Now they're made of plastic.) It's not just a handful. Valerie, who works at Oakwood Cemetery, told me they've gotten almost 130 boxes from Anthony's funeral home alone. They've got eighty-three more from another place called White's. Some guy called a few years ago for the ashes of a woman who died in 1949 and they were actually still there in the storage room, waiting, but he never showed up to claim them. After a year (the law requires at least a three-month wait) Anthony takes the abandoned cartons a few miles out into the Atlantic and scatters the ashes there. He showed me a box that was scheduled for the next boat ride. It's dark brown, and it sits inside a white cardboard box, and the whole thing weighs more than I thought it would, which is about three pounds. The ashes are gray. Nothing distinguishes them from the ashes of anything else, except Anthony told me that the white bits were bone. I thought, *Maybe if I went fishing a little deeper I might find something more recognizably human.*

"Why do people leave them here?" I asked. "Sometimes they're so sad they don't want to deal with it," he suggested. Sometimes it's just the opposite. He told me the story of a guy who called him up and said, "My father just died in Good

Samaritan Hospital. Bury the son of a bitch and send me the bill." I started to wonder about all the dead and forgotten in Bay Shore. Anthony let me go through their oldest funeral ledger books, which date back to 1937. Bay Shore has wealthy inhabitants, but this particular funeral home has always buried their servants, mechanics, and gardeners. I flipped through page after page of lives summed up by what they did for a living, the people they were married to, where they were born, and where they died—by whether or not they had fought in a war, by their race and religion, by what they died of, and by how much their funeral cost and who paid the bill. A lot of funerals were billed to the Suffolk County Department of Public Welfare. I noticed that in the 1930s, it cost two hundred dollars to bury a white housekeeper, while a black housekeeper's funeral cost seventy-five dollars. Stillborn babies were rarely named and didn't get individual plots, as far as I can tell; they all went into something called the baby section. It's a funeral-home tradition to charge only for the box, so the burial of a stillborn usually cost around twenty dollars. In the thirties, most people seemed to have died at home, not in hospitals. The causes of death seemed generally more colorful than they do today—lots of people killed themselves or got hit by trains. The sample of funerals that follow took place between 1937 and 1946 and were taken directly from the ledger books. Sometimes the entries had local newspaper articles attached.

Handyman, aged 43. Cause of death: *general paralysis of the insane.* No spouse or children. Mother unknown. Cost of funeral: $259.

Laborer, aged 83. Cause of death: *exhaustion.* Contributory cause: *senility.* Cost of funeral: $185.

Retired attendant at New York State Hospital, World War I veteran, aged 47. Cause of death: *gas poisoning, suicide*. No spouse, parents unknown. Cost of funeral: $419.

Housekeeper, aged 71. Cause of death: *exposure*. She was found on the corner of 3rd Avenue and Cherry Street. Irish widow. Cost of funeral: $75.

Retired lawyer, aged 58. Cause of death: *skull fracture caused by a train at the 5th Avenue crossing*. "He was hard of hearing," a newspaper report read. Irish widower, he lived alone and had five daughters. Cost of funeral: $325.

Female torso, white, age unknown. Cause of death: *unknown*. The newspaper said it was found on the ocean side at Camp Cheerful. Cost of funeral: $30.

Negro, aged 21. Cause of death: *drowned at Sands Point*, buried in town plot. Cost of funeral: $75.

Chauffeur, aged 42. Cause of death: *skull fracture caused by a train at the Edgewood crossing*. His truck was carrying a load of fish, according to the attached article. Cost of funeral: $35.

Eight people from the Hattie family died in one six-year period.

Hattie 1, aged 48. *Cardiovascular renal disease*. Cost of funeral: $75.

Hattie 2, aged 3 months. *Acute purulent pyelitis*. Cost of funeral: $25.

Hattie 3, aged 21. *Drowned*. Cost of funeral: $75.

Hattie 4, aged 1 month. *Intestinal obstruction*. Cost of funeral: $20.

Hattie 5, aged 6 months. *Tuberculosis*. Cost of funeral: $40.

Hattie 6, aged 1 hour, 37 minutes. *Prematurity*. Cost of funeral: $25.

Hattie 7, aged 1 hour. *Prematurity*. Cost of funeral: $15.

Hattie 8, aged 21. *Cardiovascular*. Cost of funeral: $75.

Building contractor, aged 67. Cause of death: *skull fracture caused by a train at the 3rd Avenue crossing*. "It was raining," read the newspaper report. Cost of funeral: $350.

Housekeeper, aged 50. Cause of death: *drowned in the Great South Bay while fishing and while her husband was asleep in the cabin down below*. Parents unknown. Cost of funeral: $15 for removal and preparation.

I don't understand how parents could be listed as "unknown" when the spouse is still alive. How can all these people not know who their spouse's parents were? And why does the ledger note all the stillborn Catholic babies who were specifically buried in unconsecrated ground? Catholics used to say if you died unbaptized you couldn't go to heaven, you went to limbo, and that therefore you couldn't be buried in ground that's been blessed. Every child who learns about this practice reacts with the same initial horror: "But what about the babies?" One infant died due to "premature birth caused by shock from burns." The ledger provides no other details except that she was buried in unconsecrated ground. They don't do this anymore. The Catholics took it back, the way they took back no meat on Fridays and hell. I wonder if they returned to bless all the separate, unconsecrated plots?

Housekeeper, Negro, aged 34, and stillborn infant. Cause of death: *toxemia of pregnancy*. Contributory causes: *dead fetus.* The ledger states that this was her seventh child. They were both buried in the town plot. Cost of funeral: $75.

Laborer, World War I veteran, aged 42. In the death notice it says "heart attack," in the funeral home records it says "syphilis." The Veterans Bureau paid for him to be buried in the "colored section." Cost of funeral: $100.

Clerk, aged 19. Cause of death: *gas poisoning, suicide.* The attached newspaper article says that although he had been in good spirits lately, he had been depressed about a heart condition he was left with as a result of rheumatic fever from two years before. He was popular in high school; he had graduated the previous June. He killed himself in September. No cost is listed for his funeral.

Housekeeper, aged 56. Cause of death: *suicide incurred by breathing gas from a gas stove in her home at Bay Shore while mentally deranged.* Cost of funeral: $387.

Laborer, aged 40. Cause of death: *skull fracture caused by a train at the 3rd Avenue crossing.* The watchman yelled a warning, the newspaper account read, but he walked directly into the path of the train anyway. Cost of funeral: $345.

Infant, aged 1 year, 10 months. Cause of death: *drowned in the Great South Bay by her mother, who was found insane and committed to Pilgrim State Hospital.* Her husband said she was in a highly nervous state because the child had been born prematurely, the newspaper reads. She dressed herself and the baby in bathing suits, waded out waist deep, and later told her husband that she lost the child. At her arraignment she asked three questions: Could she go home with her mother? What was the penalty for first-degree murder? And, Could she see her baby? Cost of funeral: $204.19.

Carpenter, aged 59. Cause of death: *suicide by shooting himself with a .22-caliber rifle while mentally deranged.* An article explains that he lost three fingers in an accident while on the job. After losing his house, his wife, and his savings, he went to live with his sister and brother-in-law to help them with their chicken farm. Cost of funeral: $133.

Laborer, aged 29. Cause of death: *drowned while dumping snow from his highway truck into the Great South Bay.* Cost of funeral: $360.

Housekeeper, aged 70. Cause of death: *suicide by asphyxiation incurred by hanging.* Her daughter found her hanging from the rafters of their staircase, the article states. Cost of funeral: $225.25.

Black female laborer. Cause of death: *abscesses in peritoneal cavity, lungs, kidney, and spleen, said to have followed induced abortion 29 days earlier.* Cost of funeral: $557.

Infant girl. Cause of death: *monstrosity.* Cost of funeral: $15.

The list goes on and on. Suicide by inhaling illuminating gas while "mentally deranged"; children suffocating in their bedding; people trapped in burning buildings; a newborn's cause of death is listed as "obesity." I would imagine it's the same in every town, but the number of suicides seemed high. And there was plenty of cirrhosis of the liver. And what is it with the people of Bay Shore getting run over by trains? Oh no. I'll probably die by getting hit by a train because of saying that. We've got an ongoing conversation in the Secret Space in which we point out ironic last words, the kind where if you die

117

people will say, "Isn't that funny, because they just said [for example], 'If I'm lying may God strike me dead.' " That type of thing. I'll get hit by a train and people will point to this paragraph and say, "Isn't it funny? Because she *said* she was going to get hit by a train." If I were there to comment, I'd add, "Yeah. What an idiot."

work

I HAVE JUST MADE a horrifying discovery about my new crush, Seth Green, from *Buffy the Vampire Slayer*. He's twenty-four. Twenty-four. Is this what I have to look forward to? Crushes on twenty-four-year-olds until I'm eighty-five? I didn't like twenty-four-year-olds when *I* was twenty-four. And this is my life. I wake up in a good mood on Tuesday mornings because Tuesday night is *Buffy the Vampire Slayer* night. Life is good because of a television show, and I'm not just saying that. As I've said before, I could live for TV, I am that shallow. I choose to live on the surface because there's nothing good at the bottom. What is good is on top, right where I want it, and where I can keep an eye on it. Underneath is where I hide everything I can't bear to look at too closely or for too long. Such as why, for example, a TV show is the highlight of my week.

Luckily, I have a Plan B for my life and what I'll do if Echo

119

goes under before I can find the right buyer. It's perfect. It addresses both my being sick of new media and my need to find a job that doesn't involve billing people. It involves working on the surface. I'll work in television. I'll develop a show about Echo and cyberspace and call it *Virtually Yours*. I'll write about all the psychodramas online and between the people who have to deal with them back at the office. It'll be *Ally McBeal* on the Internet. A career in television would be perfect for me. I love television. I should create it. I know how naive that sounds. It's like someone who has never painted before proclaiming they're going to produce *Starry Night*. Still. In a *TV Guide* interview, David Chase, the creator of *The Sopranos*, said television "attracts people who are determined to be miserable." Home. Maybe working in television will replace the low-level panic that has gripped me for so long that it's turned me into a tuning fork for fear—tap me to hear what note terror sings. Television is not going to go away, unlike Echo. And no one is going to threaten to pee voluminously at me because of his cable bill. That would be someone else's problem. Part of the fantasy—I mean, *plan*—is that I will find people like me in TV Land and maybe one of them will be the man of my dreams. Okay, not Seth Green, he's too young, but how about Joss Whedon, the creator of *Buffy the Vampire Slayer*, or David Greenwalt, the co–executive producer? Which brings me to the heart of the matter. Who the hell are Seth Green and Joss Whedon and David Greenwalt and why am I writing about them? Because I'm an idiot and I hate myself. And because I'm the kind of person who's comfortable in an imagined, distant world.

Going to work in television would be like getting a job on my home planet. Everything would snap into place: the dead would be redeemed, justice restored, and the meaning and purpose of life revealed in all their balanced glory.

I actually went to the Web site for *Buffy the Vampire Slayer* to see if any of the guys on that show—because they're all adorable, I'd take any one of them—are anywhere near my age. Why do I do this? Why must my fantasy life be rooted in reality? Like it really matters how old Seth Green is. Like I really have a shot. But I took time out of my day and clicked on every picture of every guy in the show to find out how old they were. I'm the George Costanza of middle-aged women. (And Anthony Stewart Head, the actor who plays Giles on *Buffy the Vampire Slayer*, is my man.)

I know how that sounds, but actually it's worse. When I go to parties and meet someone who works in television, the conversation goes like this.

ME: Oh! You have the best job.

They don't say anything at first. They're speechless, but not a good speechless.

ME: What, you don't like TV?
THEM: You do?
ME: Well, yeah. *Buffy!*
THEM: Oh. Will you excuse me, please? I see an old friend I'd like to say hello to.

The FBI once came by my office. A hacker was using our computers as a jumping-off point to break into some other computers in California. They had called to arrange a meeting. "We'd like to come to your office to speak with you. Would that be all right?" they asked me. "Only if you look like Mulder or Scully," I answered.

So I have reality issues. But I'm not completely insane. I know that working in television won't solve all my problems or eliminate all my fears. I'm just hoping it will involve the kinds of problems and fears that go underneath so fast I barely register their existence. If only. One of the curses of midlife—

after years of watching in horror as I make the same mistakes over and over, I already know that wherever I go, whatever job I find myself doing, even if it all looks very different at the beginning, I will in time come back to the same place. I learn nothing. My life is in permanent rerun.

Television is like going home. On TV, no one dies, nothing changes. I can run across *Starsky and Hutch* or *The Little Rascals* the way I ran across Olive Huber's gray, fishlike appendix. It will always be there, right where I left it, and I can think, *Still here, still here, still here,* saved by the world of my undead, night-light friends.

On the other hand, if I did get a job in television I might implode. I'd be parachuting straight into my daydreams, which would make them reality, bringing close what had been safely distant. I would be like Lewis Carroll's Alice, reaching through the silver of the Looking Glass and shaking hands with the Alice on the other side. Stacy and Anti-Stacy—or Imagined Stacy—would meet. One would have to go. Stacy and Anti-Stacy would annihilate each other. If only they could merge. Wouldn't that be a nice, happily-ever-after ending? Which means, of course, that it will never, ever happen.

Given that I am totally deluding myself, what problems would arise when a person like me, someone who lives half in reality and half in daydreams, goes to work in television? Television is a fantasy within a fantasy, removing me that much further from what's lurking underneath. I wouldn't just be living on the surface, I would be floating a few inches above it. How painful would my awakening be?

poLL

From a poll of 136 people on Echo:

*Name one thing you hope to accomplish before you die,
something that will bug you on your deathbed if you don't.*

Sixteen percent said publish a book.
Thirteen percent said have a child.

Not everyone asks much of life. A few favorites:

"I want to NOT go to DC ever again. I want to die
without ever going to DC."
"Since getting out of debt is on the horizon, I'd like to
use up all my fabric."

"Finish something. Completely. Done. Handed in. And I don't mean dying."

A mere 8 percent said "find someone to love," or, as one person put it, "To infatuate one person who isn't hideous, psycho, or crippled."

cats

HAD THE FOLLOWING CONVERSATION with Veets and Beams while I was giving Beams his .9 percent sodium chloride subcutaneous drip.

ME (TO BEAMS): Who's the greatest cat in the whole wide world?

BEAMS: [Silence.]

ME (TO BOTH): Well, they took a vote. It was a worldwide vote and it was very close—there are a lot of great cats in the world, you know—but in the end it was a tie. You and Veets won.

ME (TO BEAMS): And you won the World's Best Subcutaneous-Drip-Taking Cat Award.

ME (TO BOTH): Don't tell all the other cats about these awards, though. We don't want them to feel bad.
VEETS/BEAMS: [Silence.]

[VEETS MOVES IN FOR SOME ATTENTION. I PET HIM.]

ME (TO VEETS): I'm sure if you had to, you'd be a great Subcutaneous-Drip-Taking cat, too.
VEETS: [Silence.]

Then I sing Beams the song from the Debbie Reynolds/Eddie Fisher movie that I rent every Christmas, *Bundle of Joy*. It's a bluesy kind of lullaby and Debbie Reynolds sings it to a baby that is left on her doorstep. It begins, "How I love my pretty baby, sweet and precious pretty ba-a-a-by." Veets and Beams have never given me any indication of whether they like me to sing to them, but for purely selfish reasons I opt for the they-like-me-to choice.

ME (TO BOTH): Would you like a cup of coffee? [I always give Beams his drip in the morning.]
BEAMS/VEETS: [Silence.]
ME (TO BEAMS): Almost done.
ME (TO VEETS): Isn't your brother brave? [They're not brothers by birth, but I call them that.]
ME (TO BEAMS): My Lailey cat! [Another one of the million nicknames I have for them. Munchkin-Munchkalailey-Lailey.]

Beamers tries to get up. The drip is running slowly this morning and his subcutaneous-drip-taking tolerance has reached its limit. To calm him, I lean in close and breath warm air onto his head. Then I pet him just above the eyes and on the sides of his face. Veets comes over and licks the top of his head. He always steps in to do that at just the right

126

moment. It can't be accidental. He knows when Beamers is upset.

When you give cats insulin injections, they don't even flinch. If they're purring, the purring won't stop when the needle goes in. This needle is different. It's huge. I guess the point is to get the fluid in fairly quickly, but it's so big that I feel like I'm stabbing Beamer. Unlike with the insulin syringe, there's resistance. You have to shove. Beamers jerks. Once it's in he seems to be okay, but still . . . it takes some getting used to. For both of us.

Beamers's fur around the needle rises up into a small ball that will disappear as the solution spreads. When I see this ball, it means we're almost done.

ME (TO BEAMS): Almost done, hon.

Veets sticks his paw in my face. He's not getting enough attention.

ME (TO VEETS): What a patient Boo-Cat.
ME (TO BEAMS): You're a patient Boo-Cat, too. Who's the Most Amazing Subcutaneous-Drip-Taking Cat in the whole wide world?

There is a joke that goes: Cats are a lonely woman's excuse to talk to herself. Wonderful. There's some truth to this but, really, what have I got to be ashamed of? I love my cats. They make me happy. Cleveland Amory talked to his cat. But Cleveland Amory had a bit of that crotchety-old-bachelor thing going, and it's okay for crotchety old bachelors to fall in love with their cats. And it's okay for gay men. If a straight man my age talked to his cats, he would be considered charming. Why do they get to be charming, and me (and all women) pathetic?

I tell myself that my conversations with Veets and Beams aren't pathetic because, first of all, they don't involve the baby talk most people use with their cats, and, second, they're funny. Then I think that perhaps it makes them even more pathetic. Were my conversations closer to real conversations, I'd be more deluded than women who simply babble. No, I decide, it just means we are vocally mimicking different relationships. Women who babble think of their cats as babies. I think of them as friends. Okay, so that *does* make the joke even more true. Oh, so what? Isn't everybody lonely? Women with husbands sometimes seem the loneliest of all. Nobody's got the answer. No one wins, because no one knows what winning looks like.

Once again I lean in close and I whisper to Beamers.

ME (TO BEAMS): Almost done, Beams, almost done.

work

I'VE DECIDED THAT if I can't write for television I'm going to try to correct a mistake I made twenty years ago. And if that doesn't work, I'm going to give Echo to a friend to look after and then I'm going to hit the road. A.k.a. Plans C and D. It's something I picked up working in the computer industry—multiple backup plans.

The mistake I want to correct has been bugging me since 1980. I was twenty-four at the time and had just moved back to New York after college, and after getting married far too young to someone I remain friends with to this day (we stayed married for two years). I took a job at Tiffany's because it was the only place to offer me one. I was a Christmas temp and sold jewelry at the Elsa Peretti counter on the main floor. Although I complained bitterly about the job, I secretly loved it. Tiffany's was all so civilized. From my counter I could stand around quietly and discreetly stare and stare and stare at all the kinds of people who come into Tiffany's: tourists, rich people, celebrities, and the mobs of Japanese girls who preferred silver to gold and who crowded around the Elsa Peretti counter like puppies. When Christmas was over I was asked to stay on and work full-time but I said no. I didn't think selling jewelry at Tiffany's was a "real" job. It wasn't a "career." Instead, like an idiot, I went on to work for the next ten years at one truly hateful job after another, each of which made me want to kill myself. And all because I hadn't had the nerve to say I loved the frickin' Tiffany's job.

Then I started Echo. And when I ran out of money at the end of Echo's first year, I went back to the main floor at Tiffany's. It was all so wonderfully unchanged. *Home, home, I'm home,* I thought. This time, however, they didn't ask me to stay when Christmas was over. That's because several times a day I would call Echo from behind the Elsa Peretti counter and if one of the modems didn't answer like it was supposed to, I'd cry "Gotta go!" and rush downtown to fix it.

The next job I took was at a bookstore closer to home, from where I used to run Echo. I was terrified of running into someone from Echo. I didn't think working in a bookstore sent the right message, when I was supposed to be back in an office running Echo. Whenever someone from Echo came into the store, I would rip off my "Hi, my name is Stacy" name tag and pretend to be shopping.

I didn't get my name tag off in time when Bruce Fancher from Mindvox once walked in. Mindvox was another online service in New York and it considered Echo their competitor. We weren't friendly competitors. I was the enemy. Of all people to catch me working part-time stacking books, it had to be someone from Mindvox. They never missed an opportunity to trash me and Echo, and I was sure they'd make the most of this. *Stacy Horn working in a bookstore? Echo must not be doing so well.* I felt like such a failure. His face full of malicious glee, Bruce asked, "What are you doing here?" I forget what I said but somehow I managed to change the subject. Or maybe somewhere deep inside he had a heart and let me change the subject.

It would be so nice to grow old at Tiffany's. Or, better yet, after years of wandering around America, I'd love to settle down at a gas station in the middle of nowhere and curate a museum of odd artifacts, just like Ellen Burstyn in the movie *Resurrection*. Plan E.

pOLL

From a poll of 101 people on Echo:

Are you happy? Please express your happiness level in percentages.

Some responses were quite specific.

Five percent of the time I am significantly unhappy.
One percent of the time I wish I'd gone to work for
    Citibank.

Another: "I read Russian and East European novels for a living. How can I ever be happy? If I were happy, however, I would be happy in the same way as everyone else who is happy." (Someone else is haunted by Tolstoy.)

Overall, most people say they are happy a lot of the time. (Two people on Echo are really happy: 95 percent of the time, they said.)

Forty-four percent are happy 40 percent or more of the time.
Forty-four percent are neutral 40 percent or less of the time.
Eighty-two percent said they were miserable 15 percent or less of the time.

Only 15 percent? All right, maybe. But then they're spending the remaining 85 percent of their time talking about it.

deАtН

EMMA STEWART, who died two years before I was born, wanted the exact same thing for her twilight years that I do, and she never even saw the movie *Resurrection*. She, too, dreamed of a roadstand and gas station. "Wouldn't that be the life of Riley," she asked in a 1945 article in the *Long Island Daily Record*. Instead, she became the gravedigger and caretaker for what was essentially an abandoned graveyard in Queens called Prospect Cemetery. She was the only one willing to do the work for what the Prospect Cemetery Association could afford to pay (less than eight hundred dollars yearly through 1954), and she only had two hands, after all. Prospect Cemetery contains more than a thousand documented graves, but the actual number is believed to be as high as three thousand. They're spread over four and a half acres, which even by 1945 had been ignored for many years. Emma never got that roadstand and gas station. Instead, she pulled weeds until the day she died in the spring of 1954, at age fifty-two. After her death the Prospect Cemetery Association washed their hands of the place once and for all and never hired another caretaker. It was the end of the line for the graveyard that had been the burial site of Jamaica residents for over three hundred years.

Prospect Cemetery was partially cleaned up for the bicentennial celebrations in 1976, then it fell right back into obscurity. New burials were rare and the graves were left untended. A local animal rights activist named Amy Anderson rediscovered the cemetery in 1988 while rescuing an abandoned litter of puppies. It was already so overgrown with weeds and wildflowers that she didn't realize at first she was even in a cemetery. Amy wrote down some of the names on the gravestones, picked up a phone book, and starting randomly calling people with the same last names. This led to Cate Ludlam, who may or may not be a descendant of someone buried there—she's never actually checked—and now Cate pulls the weeds at Prospect Cemetery. I'd been passing by the place on the Long Island Railroad for decades. I couldn't see the graves until Cate started weeding, roughly ten years ago. Once I could, however, whenever my train went by it I'd daydream that Prospect Cemetery was my Willoughby. I always swore I'd get off someday and go there. Taking care of an abandoned cemetery might be the true life of Riley. "You always have the sun and stars over you when you dig a grave," Emma told the *Long Island Daily Record*. (Plan F?)

With the help of my friend and bandmate Vivian, who lives in Queens and seems to know everyone, I found myself standing by the gate, shaking hands with Cate, a small, dark-haired woman with an open face who, after after ten years of clearing graves, has Prospect Cemetery practically memorized. First she took me into the Chapel of the Sisters, which stands just inside the main gate. Built from fieldstone, sandstone, and black wal-

135

nut in 1857 by her possible ancestor, Nicholas Ludlum, for his three dead daughters, Mary Cecelia, Cornelia Maria, and Mary, it hadn't been used since 1936. The chapel consists of a small room, but the ceilings are at least thirty feet high. I dodged swooping pigeons, who come in through holes in the roof and breaks in the stained glass, and noticed that the word "incorruptible" still appears in embossed gold lettering on the now-gray walls. I walked from wall to wall, avoiding spiderwebs and brushing away the feathers that cover the floor, reading the names and dates of birth and death of the sisters, who lived only to the ages of one, thirteen, and twenty-one. I dream about restoring the chapel and living in it one day—if, like Emma, I don't get the gas station and roadstand.

After a brief tour, Cate let me wander off on my own, telling me to stand my ground should any wild dogs appear. "They'll back down if you stand firm," she told me. I instantly daydreamed about taming them into sweet, sweet pets who will live, curled up and warm, inside the Chapel of the Sisters with me.

Heaven is abandoned places. There are 339 years of graves and growth in Prospect Cemetery. Weeds, briars, and wildflowers are everywhere: myrtle, mugwort, shoebuttons, daffodils, grape hyacinth, lots of ivy, and all partially shaded beneath a grove of birch, maple, and chestnut trees. The road that runs alongside, Beaver Street, isn't even on the map anymore. Just beyond Beaver Street are the tracks for the Long Island Railroad. Every time a train passed I thought, *I'm here, I'm in Willoughby*, straining to see the faces that flickered by. I felt like I'd escaped something that they haven't. Except that they were going somewhere and I was in an abandoned graveyard.

I found a familiar name at the cemetery. "In Memory of Daniel Baylis who departed this life April 18, 1830, aged 31 years, 1 month and 26 days." *Why'd they have to be so specific?* The name stood out because of the Baylises I had tracked in the Huntington High School Alumni Directory. The last Baylis, Scott Baylis, graduated in 1981. There are eight Baylises, no Sammises, buried in Prospect Cemetery. Daniel's gravestone reads:

> *This world is vain and full of pain*
> *With care and trouble sore*
> *But they are blest who are at rest*
> *With Christ for evermore.*

If you say so, Baylis family. But I don't know. Pain or no pain, I'd rather be alive than dead, and I'll bet Daniel felt a little gypped seconds before he died—if he had seconds to think about it, that is. Thirty-one years, one month, and twenty-six days of vanity and pain are not that many, after all.

I picked up a few sordid facts about Prospect's past. For example, in 1954, the skull of fourteen-year-old Alice Josephine Smith was taken from the grave she had been buried in ninety years before. Her skull is still missing to this day. I found a jaw with three teeth in it not far from her grave, but Cate said it was the jaw of a dog. The body of a three-year-old boy murdered by his mother was found during a cleanup in 1989.

I learned a little more about Emma Stewart from another *Long Island Daily Record* article. She'd been separated from her husband for five years when she talked about the sun and stars. I learned that it generally took her five hours to dig a grave, and that she worked in the evenings, during the summer, with her collie, Major. Sometimes she was helped by her oldest son, Owen, who was twenty-two at the time (1947) and who worked for Jamaica Water Supply. Her youngest, Richard, attended P.S. 40. She once said, "A gravedigger learns the living are more dangerous than the dead." I worry about identifying with her.

Next I found the records for the nearly one hundred Revolutionary, Civil, and Spanish-American War veterans buried in

Prospect Cemetery. Our country, it would seem, has a long history of forgetting its veterans. Elias Baylis, one of the Baylises buried there, died on a prison ship during the Revolutionary War, and had been a member of the Committee of Observation and Correspondence of Jamaica. This committee passed a resolution to form a company of fifty-two minutemen. Members of the company were to be dressed in linen uniforms with yellow fringe and white feathers in their hats. Talk about denial. They're sending fifty-two of their fathers, sons, brothers, and neighbors to their probable deaths, and as they sit around the table discussing this, someone suggests that they have white feathers in their hats. They take a vote.

"Okay, all those in favor of putting white feathers in their hats, raise your hands."

Hands are counted, the white feather wins, and the detail is added to the resolution. The ones who vote for the feather must feel a brief moment of satisfaction when their vote passes. A certain S. Mills was commissioned to write a song for the fifty-two soldiers, and this is what he gave them:

> Arouse my brother Minute Men;
> And let us bear our chorus,
> The braver and the bolder,
> The more they will adore us.

> Our country calls for swords and balls,
> Our drums aloud do rattle,
> Our fifer's charms arouse the arms,
> And liberty calls to battle.

Mills makes it all sound so worthwhile. "Swords and balls": how romantic. And they're going to be "adored" for marching off. But for some it would all end in the perpetually deserted Prospect Cemetery, where I strolled among fallen gravestones and periwinkle, thinking, *This kind of perpetuity isn't so bad.* Am I like Emma, more afraid of the living than the dead? Cate Ludlam, who is closer to living out my fantasy than I am, doesn't think she's living the life of Riley.

I look for but don't find any Horns. I searched through the records in the library. No Horns are buried in Prospect Cemetery, though my grandfather Peter Maynard Horn built a house for twenty thousand dollars (an impressive but not extravagant amount) within spitting distance of the place in 1926. "I'd want at least sixty thousand dollars for it now," he said in 1969. My grandfather was a lot like me and he was a lot like Olive Huber. He raised three children in the house he built on Avon Road, leaving it only when he and my grandmother became too old to care for it. I was hoping to find a Horn in Prospect Cemetery because that would make Prospect Cemetery more like home—and that would make my fantasy just a little bit less, I don't know, *insane.* While I like my fantasies to be constrained by reality, I am a bit concerned about this one. There aren't any people in it. Am I preparing for a future as a sterile flower? "You can work in the daylight if you're afraid of ghosts," Emma said. I'm not afraid of ghosts. I'm comforted by them. Sonya attached herself to a home. I attached myself to a graveyard.

deAtH

MY FRIEND MIKAL told me not long ago that he believes my apartment is inhabited by the ghost of a woman who died with a broken heart. My first reaction: *Miss Havisham*. Which I found interesting, because even though Mikal has seen ghosts his whole life and talks about them in his first book, he also claims he doesn't believe in them.

MIKAL: But you've got one there. Definitely. I rarely feel these things anyplace.
ME: If it's not a ghost, what is it?
MIKAL: There might be ghosts in the world, but I think a lot of them are also projections. They're manifesta-tion of our horrible secrets or pains or desires, a culmi-nation of history. I don't know. My mother believed in ghosts. I think it was easier for her to make that history

something supernatural and outside of herself. It was easier for her to decide that a proverbial demon had attached itself to my brother [Gary Gilmore, who was executed in 1977 for killing two men] and was controlling his fate as opposed to the real demon of our family's cruelty.

Mikal had waited years to tell me about my ghost because he wasn't sure how I would take the news. Then, one night on the phone, he finally brought it up. Here's the first thing he said.

MIKAL: It likes to be close to you. Have you ever felt it?
ME: Never.

I practically jump.

ME: Not once.

I immediately look all around me. I look next to me, under the desk, under the couch, I turn around and look behind me. No ghost. I don't even believe in ghosts. But I stare hard at my couch, envisioning a foggy image of a girl, something like the ghost in the movie *The Uninvited*.

ME: How close? Who is it? Or was it? Why is she here?
MIKAL: Something happened there before you lived there, something that had to do with the bedroom and a sense of being trapped.

Now, that's interesting. I don't use the bedroom. I prefer to sleep on my lovely red velvet, feather-filled couch in the living room. I really don't know why; I just feel more comfortable in the living room. I tell myself it's because sleeping's cozier on the couch.

MIKAL: Didn't you tell me you never sleep in the bedroom?
ME: I sleep in the bedroom sometimes.

*I don't believe in ghosts, I don't believe in ghosts, I don't believe
in ghosts. Really.*

MIKAL: It might take comfort in your being there. But
it also might not like the cats a lot. It might have been
shut in with some animals at some point.

Doesn't like the cats? I looked over at Veets and Beams, who,
as it happens, prefer the bedroom. "What do you know about
this?" I asked them. Their response, as usual, was "Feed us."
They jumped off the couch and trotted into the kitchen because they hoped I was talking about food.

MIKAL: And it's definitely most active at night. I remember coming over to your place one night at two or three
in the morning. I walked into your living room and you
were at your keyboard, and I swear it felt like another
person was sitting on the sofa, watching us.

Aha, I think. This is why I haven't found the man of my
dreams. He continues.

MIKAL: In your bedroom it prefers to hover or stay in
corners. I don't think it gets on the bed. Something happened. There's a reason it won't go down onto that bed.
But in the living room it likes to sit close to you. And
watch. I think it might be curious about visitors, but it
tires of them. It prefers you. It's possessive. I don't think
it would hurt you, but it might try to reach you. I think
you do something for it.
    And it doesn't want you to move from that apartment.

142

Not much danger of Veets, Beams, or me going anywhere anytime soon. It worries me how little time it took me to get used to the idea of being closely watched by a heartbroken ghost. Within ten minutes I asked Mikal, "Is there anything I can do to make it feel better?"

He told me to leave a glass of cold water out for it at night, so I do. Pretty soon after that I started saying, "Hi, ghost," whenever I walked in the door—after saying hi to Veets and Beams. Mikal freaked.

MIKAL: Don't come home and say, "Hi, ghost." You're going to scare the poor thing or hurt its feelings. Give it a name and ask if it likes that name. Like Amanda. You can call it a mysterious friend, but don't waltz in and say, "Hi, ghost!" Still, no damage done. I don't think your ghost is around in the daytime. It shows up around eleven P.M.

I told him that if my ghost had been living with me for ten years it had to have gotten used to how I am by now, and would know that I meant "Hi, ghost" in the nicest possible way.

MIKAL: Ghosts don't always know they're ghosts. Especially young ones. You have a ghost that formed its attachment there in the late fifties. Who knows when the person actually died. So your ghost has been a ghost for, say, twenty or so years. That's young in ghost terms. They feel time differently. So break it to the ghostling gently, okay?
ME: How about, "Hi, Amanda. Ever wonder why no one can see you and you don't have to eat anymore?"
MIKAL: You're going to traumatize this poor thing. Young ghosts are very confused.

I changed the subject. "What does she look like?" I asked.

143

He had only a vague idea. He wasn't even completely sure my ghost was female, although he was pretty sure.

MIKAL: I don't think it will ever show itself to you. That's not an easy thing for a young ghost.

And of course that's the first thing I want. The very first thing. My ghost died of a broken heart. Maybe, like my dead grandmother Daisy, this might make her sympathetic to me. Again I hope that if dead people have any powers, they will use them on my behalf. What do I need to do to make you show your face to me, mysterious friend?

Maybe I can find out who you were.

work

RED BURNS INVITED ME and four other women to speak at the New York Women in Communications Annual Meeting. Red's my boss at New York University, where I teach one day a week. Before the meeting, she went down the line and asked each woman what she was going to talk about—it was supposed to involve some aspect of our work in new media.

RED: What are you going to talk about?
ME: My midlife crisis.
RED: You can't talk about your midlife crisis.
ME: Yes I can.
RED: No one cares about your midlife crisis.
ME: Sure they do.
RED: What does your midlife crisis have to do with anything?

ME: I don't know.

RED: Stacy, you can't talk about your midlife crisis.

ME: It'll be okay, Red.

RED: Please don't talk about your midlife crisis.

ME: Okay.

RED: You're lying.

ME: It'll be okay, I swear.

RED: I'm putting you last.

ME: Fine.

RED: Fine.

[Pause.]

RED: Don't talk about your midlife crisis.

ME: Okay.

I talked about my midlife crisis. God, it was fun. I talked about being miserable and unsure about what I would do next, and saw countless people nod and mouth, "Me too." I'll tell you, having a crisis has its good side. You're acting out, all bets are off—you're free. And you're not alone.

deAtH

I WENT TO SEE THE MOVIE *AFTER LIFE*. In it, everyone who dies goes to a place where they have to pick one memory, and that one memory will be the only memory they take with them when they go wherever it is that dead people go. I was more affected by spending two hours picking the memory I would take with me than I was by the movie, which I only half watched because I couldn't stop choosing. Two hours of going through my life, trying to find the best moments, reliving happy memory after happy memory. I felt so impervious. Like a good-times superheroine who gets her strength from remembering the best. Bad memories bounce off my invincible, Badgley Mischka–designed uniform.

First I went back to the big moments: my first kiss, the first time I had sex, my wedding day, all my graduation days, the day I started Echo, seeing my book *Cyberville* in a bookstore for the first time. Not a lot of big moments when you get right down to it. I think I used up my big moments five minutes into the film. So I kept digging. The happy memories in the next tier were smaller.

Walking from my apartment into Harvard Square during a blizzard *because* it was a blizzard and I had never been in one before. I couldn't see more than a couple of feet in front of me. It was exhilarating. Finding people at Buddy's Sirloin Pit, my favorite restaurant. Pouring A.1 sauce all over my meat and wolfing it down while the room steamed.

Or the time I drummed on Forty-sixth Street while thousands of Brazilians watched the second-to-last-game of the World Cup on television sets positioned up and down the block. Brazil won. I sensed this as much as saw it. I turned to look at the crowd at the exact same moment they turned, as one, to look at me. Their faces were a perfect expression of hope against hope that was, for once, realized, and they exploded into joy. And for that moment, the thrill and triumph of thousands were directed at me in the form of one desire, one command—to drum.

Then there was the time we ran out of chairs in the soprano section of the Grace Church Choral Society, where I sing every Tuesday night. I had to sit in the middle, in the absolute center of the altos, sopranos, basses, and tenors. All the voices moved in and out and around me like tiny meteors of sound ricocheting around the altar. It felt like I was singing a duet with every person there.

These memories were better. They had more detail than the bigger ones, which were more of a blur. I still had over an hour left, though, and now I was down to the smallest moments. But there were thousands of them.

I'm sixteen years old and sitting on the couch, waiting for Chris Baker to come and pick me up for our first date, and his face, when he arrives, is as bright and as excited as mine.

Beamers is in the cat hospital and I'm looking at his chart. It reads, "Feed Beamers when his owner visits. He eats better when she's there."

Joe and I are having a conversation that consists of our taking turns saying the (made-up) word "poat" over and over, until our stomachs ache from laughing.

It's raining so hard and fast all the drains on New York Avenue are overflowing and the puddles are up to my ankles and my best friend Chris and I are running through the streets, in the downpour, screaming at the top of our lungs, because there was nothing more fun in the world to do than scream in the rain.

Veets, who had gotten so fat he could no longer jump on the counter, lost enough weight that he just made it back up there to eat the pumpkin pie I'd special-ordered all for myself. "Good boy!" I shout.

I'd been playing the song "Rockville" by REM repeatedly for an hour and there's a knock on my door. *"Hello?"* my upstairs neighbor yells. "I'm sorry!" I yell back. "I'll stop playing it." "No!" he yells back. "What song is that? It's great!"

I've realized, as the people in the movie come to realize, as the writer of *After Life* clearly realized, that these small moments are the ones to choose. These are the true moments of glory. Plus, I'm not dead and I'm not in a movie: I don't have to pick just one memory. I can keep them all. I can go through all of these small memories anytime I want—and the best part is, they actually happen all the time. An endless parade of happy moments. Who knew? Who knew how little it takes? I thought it was the big things. I thought that if a lot of great stuff didn't happen I wasn't having a wonderful life. But nothing great has to happen. And, because it doesn't take much, the things I will want to remember forever could happen at any time.

Wait a minute. That also means it doesn't take much to

make a perfectly awful moment either. But the thing is, when I gave my life my complete and undivided attention, I couldn't remember anything bad. Not a single thing.

I'm going to meet some friends for drinks. We may not do or say anything spectacular, and yet some small thing might happen, something that might be better and more memorable than anything else that has ever happened to me before.

MUSIC

THERE'S A MOMENT in Bach's *Missa Brevis,* an exquisite moment. It comes again and again: the music arrives at these two beautiful chords, played lightly and quickly; the piece seems to pause for just a second, as if holding its breath before going on. In reality, it doesn't pause. The piece moves forward without the slightest hesitation, not even for a split second. There's no ritard. It goes right on to the next phrase.

This pains me. I want those notes to hold out a little longer—they are just so moving. A few seconds is not enough. I want them to stay. But if these chords were held longer, they would lose all their glory. The timing has to be what it is. The notes lead in, then up, then down, effortlessly, without straining, but intensely lifting, then letting go. If they didn't end, and if the music didn't move on, it would never achieve this achingly perfect moment that you want to last forever. It absolutely must end or it wouldn't be in the first place. It must end.

That's life, no? Except—and this is a very big "except"—when the *Missa Brevis* gets to the end I can hit replay over and over and over. And I do. What makes the ending of that perfect moment bearable is that I can have it again. Anytime I want. When I get to the end of my life I won't be able to hit replay.

deАtH

NOT LONG AFTER MY VISIT to Prospect Cemetery, Cate Ludlam asked if I would come back and help her weed. It was getting hard to see the graves again and she was rounding up volunteers. I'm ashamed to admit that I did give some thought to how I might get out of it: allergies (total lie), back problems (not a total lie), and of course, the cats. *They're sick and I have to stay home and keep an eye on them because I may have to rush them to the hospital*, I thought of telling her. But I couldn't forget the pleasure I had had wandering around inside the cemetery, and Cate was the one who'd got me there. I had to go.

I was late. Cate's collection of volunteers—firemen, their families, and a few people she'd found by looking around on the Internet—were already furiously clipping away. *Oh, God*, I thought, *let's get this over with*. I opened the gate and asked Cate what she'd like me to do. She put me to work on the fence. I had to clear every weed and every tree for the entire length of the fence. I perked up, because at least I might get to operate a chain saw. I'd never chain-sawed anything. It was terrifying. A chain saw is this heavy, loud, maniacally shaking, destroying thing, and you have to put your whole body into it to get it to cut down even a little tree, which felt awful. Never again.

I started clipping. Four or five hours later I came out of my trance. Now I knew why my few friends who have gardens were so obsessed. It's not work. You disappear into the roots and plants and leaves. The smell alone is hypnotic. Gardening is like resting with the earth, except not like death; closer to a good night's sleep, because you wake up from it feeling refreshed. I had to make myself stop for lunch. Then I had to make myself stop for the day. "Anytime you want me to come back, I'll come back," I told Cate. When I didn't hear from her, I e-mailed her. "So, are you going to arrange a weeding weekend again?"

In the spring of 1953, Emma Stewart, the former caretaker of Prospect Cemetery, told the *Long Island Daily Press*, "I have one pair of clippers but that's like fighting an atomic war with a bow and arrows." Forty-six years later it still feels like that. She kept at it, though, and I'm convinced she didn't have to force herself. It's a war you hope never ends. I want always to be able to go back there, to vanish into the tangle of ivy and vines and briar and clear a path to every grave, then clear out the weeds around the stone so I can read who's buried there. I'm going to bring them back, one person at a time. It will be like reclaiming ashes left in a storage closet.

I would worry about how much I love working in Prospect Cemetery were it not for the fact that I've never been happier since I started indulging my every death whim. God help me, I'm happy. My friend Liz says I'm digging a hole. I'm spending all my time preparing my grave. I feel as if I've been buried all my life and finally, at long last, I am digging myself out. Cate asked me to serve on the board of directors of Prospect Cemetery and I said yes.

cats

I'M HAPPY TO BE ABLE TO say that Beamers *used* to be my favorite cat. I used to sniff his head more than I did Veets's,
pet him a few seconds longer, and panic just a tiny bit more
whenever he was sick. Veets, on the other hand, used to have
dandruff. His fur was oily and coarse. Plus he smelled funny.
He was less affectionate, except when Beamers stayed in the
hospital. I think it all goes back to Beamers's first week home.
He was so sick that he almost didn't make it. I had to nurse
him back to life, and Veets helped because Veets is a generous
cat. He immediately adopted the big brother role with Beamers. He cleaned him and let him have the choice spots around
the house. It was great that Veets and Beams loved each other,
and that Veets was so wonderful about the situation, but that
only made me feel worse about the imbalance in my feelings.
It was so unfair. Veets was my first. I remember him as a tiny

kitten, climbing up the side of the bed, paw over paw. It was such a long journey for him, and he was doing it just in order to curl up and sleep beside me. So once a day I made myself get down on the floor to give him extra time. It wasn't that I didn't love him—I did—but I couldn't deny that my feelings for Beamers were stronger. I thought giving Veets more time would make up for this. What it did was make me love him just as much.

This made him blossom. His dandruff went away. His fur became softer. He lost weight, which meant I could gradually reduce his insulin. All of this only reinforced my new-and-improved love, which made his coat even shinier. I think I always loved Veets this much, but Beamers was so sick, and needed so much of my attention, that I had to wrap myself up in him in order to keep up with all the pills and injections and urine tests and blood tests and insulin injections.

I'm protective of Veets now. I'm hurt when others don't appreciate his wonderfulness. He was always such an angel at the vet's. Everyone commented on it. "You have such a great cat," they'd say. You could give Veets shots, take his blood, anything, and there was never a problem. He was very patient. I was so proud that Veets was nice to everyone and not a green-dot cat.

A green-dot cat is a hostile cat. At my vet they put a green dot on the chart to advise people who work with hostile cats to put on these metal mesh gloves, which look like something out of King Arthur, before handling them. Really hostile cats get two green dots. Veets and I always felt superior to the green-dot cats and their owners. I secretly believed that non-green-dot cats and their owners were somehow mentally healthier.

Everything changed the day I brought Veets in with a severe case of constipation. They had to give him two enemas to free up the blockage. When I came to pick him up, I watched them don the Camelot gloves before putting him back in his carrier. I grabbed his chart. There it was: a big, fat, shiny, new green dot. But come on—two enemas? Who could blame him? Alas, Veets has never forgotten those two enemas or forgiven the vet for them. He's been a green-dot cat ever since. I feel bad watching everyone approach him warily. "He's a wonderful cat, really," I tell them. I want them to go back to saying, "Oh, you have the sweetest cat," not "I'm sure he's very sweet with you."

I'm glad Veets and I are close now. He's healthier than Beamers. We're going to be together longer. Veets will have me all to himself again someday. And I owe him. He deserves that time when he won't have to give up the good spots. When he can curl up next to me and never have to move again.

NoſtaLgia

A FEW WEEKS AFTER the Veterans' Day parade I went to a ben-
efit for wounded bald eagles that was held on Pier 63, on
the Hudson River. The event was hosted by the singing veteran Rick Carrier and the USA Bald Eagle Command, and I
went for two reasons. One, I think the man I'm looking for is
also drawn to people and parties like this, and two, I couldn't
forget Rick Carrier and his smile and the way he had such a
good time singing "Bye, Bye Blackbird" on an almost empty
stage. It was cold on the river and about to rain and no more
than twenty people were there when I arrived. I spotted Rick
right away. He had on a navy blue uniform this time instead of
a brown one. Up close, I realized he was not as young as I had
thought, though in good shape for someone seventy or more.
So he must be a World War II vet, not a Korean War vet. Big-

band music was playing on a cassette player, but no one was dancing. They were grilling salmon. I left. I didn't know these people and I felt uncomfortable.

And now I hate myself. Here's the thing about middle age—you know that when an opportunity presents itself, it may be your last chance. Why didn't I stay? What did I do instead? I went home and watched reruns on TV.

Weeks earlier, when Rick and I and the few other people got up on the stage to sing after the Veterans' Day parade, we were singing for no one. No one. The cops were watching us because there was nothing better to look at. Same with the people forced to smoke on the street because of the smoking laws.

Things were different fifty-some-odd years ago. On V-E Day, Rick would have been singing along with millions of people in Times Square, and they would have sung any song he wanted them to sing. That joy has been gone for some time now. The moments of glory in between don't come so often anymore. Now, except for the cops, a few elderly women, and one middle-aged woman, me, plus whatever friends are still alive, no one notices what Rick sings.

And I may never have another chance to feel awkward at a gathering of a few shivering strangers trying to build homes for broken birds. Nothing lasts—not love or life or gratitude, and definitely not opportunity. I take that back. Regret lasts. Why didn't I go up to Rick and say hello when I had the chance? What will ever make the limits of life bearable? There I was, sitting back at home, in my good jeans, with my hair all done up special. Why did I go home when my heart was full of hope and longing?

A month later I sent a tiny contribution to Rick Carrier's foundation for injured bald eagles. I decided to track him down and ask him the questions I'd been asking other elderly people.

But he didn't answer at the number I had for him, or another number the United War Veterans Council gave me. There was an address for his group, the USA Bald Eagle Command. *I'm going to walk over there and see what I find*, I decided.

What if Pier 63 really was my last chance?

romance

M AURO'S SHIRT DOESN'T SMELL ANYMORE. I put it in the closet to hide it from the woman who comes in to clean my apartment, because I was afraid she'd wash it, and then I forgot all about it. Mauro and I don't sleep together anymore. I pulled his shirt out when he sent me the first e-mail he'd sent in a long time, and now it doesn't smell like him; it smells like the wood it's been lying next to for . . . Then it hits me. I haven't slept with anyone in a year. What have I been doing with myself? Why am I sniffing shirts instead of boyfriends?

It doesn't help that many of the women I know are in the same boat. Except Ivana Trump and Marla Maples have no problem finding boyfriends, and aren't they kinda gross? Okay, there's money. Plus the trophy thing for men in their circle, who don't find them gross . . . that's it. I haven't found the right circle. I have to find the circle of men who think someone like me is a catch. The problem is I'm already living the life that I want to be living—SOB's and cemeteries—so, technically, I've already made my debut to the men of my circle. I haven't been out there trying to land the men who would date Ivana and Marla.

Joe suggests, very practically, "Why don't you get Mauro to put his shirt on so it smells like him again?" I want a real boyfriend, I tell him. Not the olfactory traces of one.

But I'm hopeful. Maybe I just need new circles. Maybe as I search for my ghost and my dead relatives and Rick Carrier I'll find some guy digging in the same corners I am.

Inside my head:

And he'll look just like George Clooney.

*Okay, he doesn't have to look like George Clooney, but it would
be great if he could sing as well as George Clooney's aunt.*

Wait. No. I take that back. It's okay if he can't sing.

Great. Now you've jinxed it.

Right. A jinx. That's my problem.

deAtH

I THINK OUR BODIES drug us as we age. While we slow down in preparation for death, our bodies release some chemical that makes us not care as much about things we cared about when we were twenty. A physical shift takes place so gradually that we hardly notice. I remember when I was in my twenties I'd be in a good mood all day if I knew I had a party to go to that night. If I'd gotten the invitations then that I receive now, I would have had to be sedated, I'd have been so excited. What I was going to wear would occupy my thoughts for the entire day. *Those cute leather boots that come up to my ankle, or heels?* Now I throw the invitations out. My friends and I talk with genuine pride about not partying the way we used to.

Further evidence that I'm winding down: I read in the Secret Space on Echo about all the things my younger friend Rachel is doing with her life—all these classes, job leads, dates. "No flies on you, Rachel," I write. Me, I'm covered with flies. Regular old houseflies that I've made into pets. They all have names; seventeen of them have diabetes, and I'm giving them regular insulin injections. I didn't even notice that I'm not out and about the way I used to be until I read about Rachel. My aging body is lulling me toward the end. "Watch some TV," it says. *Okay.*

I didn't even like my twenties, really. I was miserable. The twenties were such a manic pinball game of emotions. Either I was crying and putting on music I knew would keep me crying, or I was ecstatic and putting on music in order to dance and work myself up into an even bigger happy frenzy. I used to dance in my apartment before I went out. Now I don't. More evidence.

I'd like to be able to say that the forties are so much better because they're calmer, and they are better in many ways, but I can't lie. I want to be in a good mood all day again because I have a party to go to tonight. And while I feel liberated by not caring about what I wear, it really is a relief—fashion is a lot of work—but that's all it is. A relief. Less work, not more fun. I have happily sacrificed fun for a little peace.

I remember crying from a broken heart when I was twenty-five. I was in agony. I sat in the middle of the living room floor and rocked back and forth, right on the edge of not being able to bear it, which is just what went through my head. *I can't bear it, I can't bear it, I'm not going to make it,* I thought melodramatically, as only a twenty-five-year-old can. I didn't want to feel what I was feeling. I remember praying to the God I don't believe in, to make me never feel that bad again. And I never do feel that bad anymore, but I regret it. And the high from the love that preceded the agony. I miss it.

I take it back. I was only twenty-five. What did I know?

Then again, it's not like I can do anything about this progression. Maybe it's better that I don't feel so keenly the gradual loss of everything I once had. The dizzying scent I loved from Mauro's T-shirt is gone.

MUSIC

GRACE CHURCH GLOWS under the sodium vapor lights. From across the street, it looks like an orange Oz. Behind the towers, brilliant white clouds rush past like a movie playing at high speed. Inside, immediate relief. I always feel better in here. It's so dark, deep, and solid. It almost feels permanent. I've been singing with the Grace Church Choral Society for close to twenty years. Sometimes I think singing inside Grace Church with the Choral Society is as close to redemption as I'm ever going to get. I look up. What's up there, anyway? A second row of stained-glass windows, but you can't see what they depict. Saints, presumably. Who picked the saints that you can't see? Are they somehow lesser saints?

John, our director, tells us to take our places, and we go through a door at the back of the church to stand in front of the altar, just behind the orchestra. I make sure I get a spot next to the tenors because I prefer to stand next to a part different from my own—I feel as if I'm singing a duet. The lights are low but it's not completely black; it's more like dusk. I can make out the aisles and the pews, but they're not distinct. I like to imagine that the dead dance in the aisles of Grace Church when we sing just right, when we hit the glory notes.

Glory notes are just what you think they would be. I don't know how it happens, but your throat just opens up; something in your chest vibrates and everything is easy after that. The best notes just come. They sound more pure, more to the point, more spit-it-out clear, and while I have no idea how you get there, it's effortless once you do. You may not be a great singer, but when you hit the glory notes, your singing is as good as it gets. When a truly great singer hits the glory notes, you cry.

We sing an entire Respighi piece—*Lauda per la natività del Signore*—once through to see how we sound with the orchestra. Heads up, eyes on John, very intent, we do our best. John says, "Good start," and points out where it went wrong. We nod. The dead are shivering in the stone, waiting for us to release them.

We begin again. I'm not there yet. No glory notes. Then Andy, a tenor standing next to me, hits them. I lean in as close as I can without touching him. Such exquisite pleasure. He sways as he sings and his shirt brushes my arm. Sometimes I can feel his shoulder under the cloth. The rest of the choir sounds like it's singing from a little ways away. I can't make the dead dance yet, but Andy can. Slowly, from all around the church, they start rising from the stone and wood and glass. They fly up and out, like water from a fountain. There are dozens of them. Dozens more are drifting down from corners I can't see clearly. Andy keeps singing and singing and the dead start to blaze, as if his voice were electricity running to some inner filament that responds to just the right song, just the right current. I keep leaning into Andy. I lean in as close as I think

166

I can get away with, as close as I can to his lovely voice. When he brushes against me I wonder if it's accidental or deliberate. Then something in me relaxes, lets go, and my voice breaks free and I'm off, I'm there. The whole choir is there.

The sounds we make! It feels like they're coming from somewhere in, yet below, our chests, and inside our heads—growing, pushing, still pushing, then leaving and hitting the room, flutelike, mixing with all these other voices. So easy. We have to do little more than open our mouths and breathe.

Now the church is white, bright, and alive with ghosts and color. I feel like Dorothy stepping out of her tornado-flung farmhouse and into shards of light shining down like spotlights—gold bands, blue bands, rosy bands, colors everywhere, all dusty and deceptive; they look so solid, as if you could climb them straight up to heaven.

The dead couples call out to me as they dance by. I like to dream that they are saying, "There are worse things than death." Their faces have a dark amber glow, an excited glow, like looking through the air above a fire. They're wearing gowns and tuxes, yards of silk, satin, taffeta and jewels and pearls and ribbons, everyone and everything swirling in a lustrous, radiant light. Everything's blazing so bright it's almost hard to see. "There are worse things than death." My reality requirement goes right out this window with this fantasy, but that's okay, because it's not that kind of fantasy. I'm dreaming about the afterlife. I can make up whatever I like.

There isn't enough room for all the dead, so some float up to dance around the chandeliers that hang in two lines, one on either side of the center aisle. The lights look like candles and I'm afraid the dead will go up in flames, but of course they're dead and the lights aren't really candles and this whole thing isn't real, so I stop worrying about that.

A couple of hours later the singing stops. It feels almost physically painful. The rehearsal is over and we have to discuss the performance tomorrow night—who's wearing what, arrival times, the order of the pieces we're going to sing. Plans are made for a party after. The colors, light, and dancing slow like a record winding down. Maybe I only think I sang better. It always feels like you sound better when you sing next to someone with a better voice. I talk to Andy, and his speaking voice and his manner are as graceful as his singing. I'm glad. It would really wreck the whole effect of the evening if they weren't. He's so beautiful, but married, and I wonder when oh when will I ever freaking luck out and find my own Andy. I don't want to go home. But everyone is packing up. I can't just stand here. I have to leave. It's over. Relentlessly, indifferently over.

I turn my head once more to look into the church, and they're all back. Dozens and dozens of dead people dressed to the nines, heavy with eternity and imaginary jewelry and with nothing to do but dance.

pOLL

F<small>ROM A POLL OF</small> 140 <small>PEOPLE ON</small> E<small>CHO:</small>

What do you want more than anything else?

Thirty-four percent replied, "True love."
Twenty-one percent replied, "Inner peace or contentment."
Sixteen percent replied, "A home."

I think the people who didn't say "true love" didn't because they've already found it. One person replied, "I want my body back," and that scared me. Another person said, "I would like to have my cat back," and that scared me even more. "She was the closest thing to a soul-mate I've found so far in this damn swift life," he continued, "and isn't that the sort of happiness any mature soul longs for?" His cat was diabetic and had recently died of kidney failure. Beamers is diabetic and has kidney disease.

I'll say, "Inner peace." That way I won't long for anything anymore.

cats

I WORRY A LOT ABOUT MY cats and the fact that their whole world
consists of two rooms, the living room and the bedroom.
Those are their choices: they can hang out in the living room
or they can hang out in the bedroom.

"Where shall we sit today? On the bed or on the couch?"

"Don't forget the floor. We could always sit on the floor."

Then, later:

"I'm tired of being in the living room. Why don't we move
to the bedroom now?"

Thirteen and fourteen years of moving back and forth, back
and forth, between only two rooms. I find this almost too awful
to contemplate. Thirteen and fourteen years of the same two
rooms: this is the life I have given them. Perhaps only country
people should have cats.

I was worrying a lot about it when it occurred to me during

Echo's weekly staff meeting, where I had raised the subject, that I obsess about this because I'm living the exact same tiny life as my cats. My whole world is two rooms: my apartment in the Village, and my office a twenty-minute walk away. When this occurred to me I was staring at a plastic, multicolored beach-ball globe that we keep around the office for dogs and children to play with when they visit. I was staring at it, thinking, *Here's this great big world, all these streets, towns, cities, countries, and continents, and I just move between my home and my office.* My space on the beach-ball world is so small it's not even represented. Back and forth, two rooms here, two rooms there, that's my whole world. *Where shall I sit today? At my desk or on the couch?* Okay, sometimes I break things up by going to NYU to teach, or to SOB's, or to Grace Church, but essentially my cats and I live in two rooms. I've got a twenty-two-block walk between my two rooms, and Veets and Beams have a thirteen-foot-long hallway between theirs.

This realization cheers me up. Because the truth is, I'm perfectly happy with two rooms. I like seeing other places but I'm not unhappy when I don't. I'm content, I told my staff. And if I'm okay with the tiny life, it's possible that Veets and Beams are okay with it, too. I should relax already. And maybe ours is not such a limited life, anyway. Maybe, I'm starting to think, the whole big, plastic, multicolored, beach-ball universe is within.

deatH

"**I**T'S GOTTEN STRONGER since the last time I was here," Mikal said as he sat down on my couch. I had asked him to come back to see if he could find out anything more about my ghost. I liked the idea of having one and wanted to know more about her, so I took this as good news.

Then I told him that I was thinking of using my bedroom again. I want to start enjoying all of my apartment. I was getting the whole place repainted. The bedroom was going to be linen white with mossy-green trim, and I'd bought new sheets and a new lamp to make it all fresh and bright.

"Not a good idea," Mikal said. "Something horrible happened in there," he reminded me.

He looked up over his right shoulder, to the corner above the window right behind him, and pointed with his chin. He was telling me that that was where my ghost was—right that second. This made conversation awkward and uncomfortable. To talk about her with her hovering there felt rude. We'd been whispering in an effort to be polite, but it wasn't working. I looked into the blue, neon-lit corner. Nothing. Mikal pantomimed talking to me on the phone. He was telling me that we'd talk later on the phone. I air-typed to indicate that we could also talk on the computer.

A couple of minutes later Mikal asked, "Can I go back into the bedroom?" "Sure," I replied, trying to sound nonchalant, as we both pointedly don't look into the corner. Now, I don't actually believe in ghosts—it's more that I'm comforted by the idea of them—but when we went back to the bedroom, I felt menace. We looked at each other and understood without speaking: *We'll talk about this at another time.*

We talked two nights later at a local club. I'm still determined that my perfectly good bedroom is not going to go to waste, but Mikal said, "Remember how little time I spent in that bedroom? She was right on top of us in the bedroom. I mean, a foot or two away at the most. It was intense." He told me again that something really bad happened in there.

Like what? "Murder? Rape?" I suggested. "Worse," he replied, dramatically. He wouldn't go into detail except to say there were things worse than murder or rape, things that go on for a long time. I tried to imagine what that might be. The only thing I could think of that might be worse would be something involving a child. When I asked him if something happened to my ghost when she was a child, he said, "Maybe."

He'd originally told me that my ghost only came at night. Now he said it was there all the time. "It watches over you. It's protective of you."

"Will it ever show its face to me?" He didn't think so.

"Will it help me?"

"If it could. If anyone ever tried to hurt you it would try." Because we were sitting in a crowded club, he was screaming his answers at me "Everyone here thinks I'm crazy because of you." I ignored him. "What color is her hair?" Dark. And she might have a slight blemish or scar. "How old is she?" Late twenties, early thirties. "How big is she?" Bigger than me, but not big. Her favorite color is red. She likes romantic music. She likes TV, but only when I'm watching it. He suggested buying her flowers, because no one had ever bought her flowers, and I did: two bunches of orange-colored daisies. "Did she like the flowers I got her?" He thought she did.

"What did she think of you?"

"She doesn't know what she thinks of me, so she's suspicious. She withdrew from me while I was there but followed me the moment I went to your bedroom to look around."

I have a very traditional image of ghosts. "When she followed you, did she walk or float through the air?"

"I don't think it's accurate to say she floats through the air—she's not wispy, she's as substantial as she wants to be, and bigger than she used to be. But no, she didn't walk."

She can't leave the building, he told me. But she might go up to the roof or onto the fire escape. I suddenly felt sorry for my brokenhearted ghost, who is bound to my two rooms, like me and Veets and Beams. Is she bound there for eternity? What else can I do for her? "Bring a child into the apartment for a visit," Mikal told me. "But what you can most do for her is live your life. She's deeply attached to your development. She is attached to your growth, struggle, changes, and hopes. She worries about you being alone so much, but she is also very watchful over anybody you bring in there."

My ghost had taken on the guardian-angel-like qualities I long for from my dead ancestors. Okay. I had to find out who she was. How hard could it be? Mikal had told me she lived there in the fifties. When I asked people on Echo how I could find out who used to live in my building, a few mentioned reverse telephone directories. Instead of looking someone up by name, you can look up a particular address, by year, and see everyone who lived there then. I knew that the Department of Housing and Community Renewal kept records of tenants in rent-controlled and rent-stabilized apartments. There had to be all sorts of ways I could track her down. Then I remembered someone telling me that my old neighbor Lotte Faderwick, who lived in this building for more than sixty years, lived in a nursing home just a few blocks away. Maybe, if I was lucky, Lotte would remember a very sad woman who lived here more than forty years ago. This was great. Someone who might have actually known my ghost. Better than a phone book listing—if I'm lucky. (And stay away from railroad crossings.)

rick carrier

BUT I HAD SOMEONE ELSE I wanted to find first. I headed over
to Grand Central and the office for the USA Bald Eagle
Command to see if I could discover what happened to my missing veteran, Rick Carrier. The address I had put the Bald Eagle
Command between Forty-second and Forty-third on Lexington. I got to within a block when suddenly he popped out of
another building, stood in front of me for a few seconds, and
then started walking east on Forty-second Street. I watched
him walk away. I hadn't seen him in a year. So I wasn't sure it
really was him. He was getting farther away. I thought I should
go to the office first. It probably wasn't him. They'd tell me
how to reach him over at the USA Bald Eagle Command. I
should go there first. He started to disappear into the crowd.
Regret and self-loathing kicked in. *Remember last year? Trying to*

look nice and walking to the docks and then walking away without ever going up to say hello?

I ran. "Hello!" I said a little too loudly. "Are you Rick Carrier?" He smiled. He was. "I was going over to the USA Bald Eagle Command to find you," I told him and then he told me that the USA Bald Eagle Command was nowhere near there. "What address do you have?" It was wrong. "I've been trying to call," I said. "What phone number do you have?" I showed him the two numbers. Wrong. Wrong. So for weeks, months, I'd been calling the wrong numbers, and there I had been heading to the wrong address and just as I hit the wrong corner, I found him.

Rick Carrier was born April 10, 1925, in Etna, Pennsylvania, and grew up watching the fireworks shoot out of the nearby factories of Tube City Steel. Flakes of iron and steel like diamond chips would float down, and everything sparkled. "You were born with pig iron in your balls," his dad, an engineer at the mill, told him. "And you ain't about to let them get rusty." Then the mill closed and his father lost his job. Rick remembers the Depression and government truckloads of cheese blocks and pecans.

Good thing about the pig iron, though. Drafted into the Army in 1943, Rick was in the first wave to hit the beaches at Normandy. "They never get the noise right," he told me. Loud. Constant. He described five-, six-, twelve-, and sixteen-inch shells flying overhead from both directions, mortar, all this aircraft, bombers, glider troops. A noisy, moving awning of death. Rick was an assault engineer, and it was the assault engineer's job to blow up obstacles and clear the area of land mines. When he made it to the seawall alive, the first thing he did was relieve himself. Right in front of Teddy Roosevelt, Jr., who was limping down the length of the wall, hitting officers in the head with his cane to get them back out and fighting. Rick noticed that Teddy was swallowing continuously. "Here." He offered

Teddy a shot of bourbon. Teddy thought he was drinking water and downed it in one gulp. His look changed from anger to happy surprise. "Thank you kindly, soldier," he said to Rick with gusto.

Rick's army career was colorful. During the war he had a brief, intense affair with a German double agent working for the American OSS. Her code name was Leni. It lasted a week and Rick never saw or heard from her again. (That's a whole other story. Or book.)

Rick met his wife Barbara when they were in college. They had two sons, Mark and Alan. Mark, an artist, died two years ago, at the age of forty-four, and Alan works in real estate. They all lived in New York while Rick worked as a producer for Embassy Pictures. He had affairs; Barbara had affairs; then he met Lynn around Christmastime 1968, when he got back from Vietnam, where he had been working as a private contractor for the Department of Defense. Rick and Barbara divorced; then Rick left the film business to write books, and he and Lynn have been together ever since.

In 1975, while he was hang gliding in Golden, Colorado, two bald eagles flew alongside Rick at eleven o'clock and five o'clock. From that moment on he was hooked. He formed the USA Bald Eagle Command to create homes for injured eagles that would otherwise be put to sleep. He recently wrote a screenplay for Eugene O'Neill's play *Anna Christie*, and he wants to have it made into a digital film.

Every year Rick Carrier marches in the Veterans' Day parade down Fifth Avenue to Madison Square Park.

Are you old?

Yes, chronologically. Spiritually, I am in my forties.

He doesn't feel old to me.

179

What are the main differences between the young you and the you now?

Physically, mentally, I'm more directed. My libido—no difference, except it's focused on one woman. No more affairs. And I'm starting a whole new career.

Did you have a midlife crisis?

No. There was the divorce and destruction of my family when I got back from Vietnam. Barbara had left me and she left me with my two teenage sons, who blamed me for everything. They didn't forgive me for thirty years.

So far no one has had a midlife crisis. Is having a midlife crisis a relatively new thing?

How do you feel when you see your body in the mirror?

Pretty good. I need to get some exercise in my arms, but my body is in good shape. My skin's a little dry.

What scares you?

Being infirm and in an old veterans' home, unable to take care of myself. If I had to go, I'd go to one in Florida or Texas.

Is there anything that no longer frightens you?

I'm not afraid of death. I got over that on the beach at Normandy. I was so close to it. As close as I am to you. When you face a critical situation, you don't spread out, you focus in. Normally I'm like the Internet. I let everyone in, I let all information in. But when I'm in danger I shut down and focus in tight. I shut the adrenaline down. That's what gets people in trouble, it fucks you up.

I was walking into my building once with two bags of groceries. Two guys came up behind me with knives and said,

"Keep walking." They were going to follow me into my apartment. I shut down; then a few seconds later I said, "I don't live here. I'm just delivering groceries."

Is there anything you no longer care about?

Failure. I don't care about failure. If someone is mad at me, or if someone is chasing me because I have a delinquent bill, it's all just paper. I got out of the film business. I was a green kid in a pack of wolves. I didn't take hold of the reins. I backed away. I went away like Chris Christopherson in *Anna Christie.*

This is comforting to hear. I've been feeling like a great big failure lately. The phone company is after me to catch up with these phone bills and they're starting to make ominous threats.

You are addressing someone you care about, someone young. Please finish this sentence. "If you only knew . . ."

. . . that you are in complete and total charge of your life; what you do with it, what you wear, what you take into your body with love and affection and honor. We're an animated sculpture. We see only the surface and we don't bother to look inside. Inside is your brain, your eyes, your stomach, intestines, sexual parts, and we're responsible for their upkeep and welfare.

You are in charge of what you are, have been, and will be, and if you do not accept this, you will become everything you do not want to become: old, decrepit, sick, arthritic, loaded with cancer. You'll have a life without people, places, friends, and most of all a life without a spiritual guide; God, Buddha, Confucius, or Jesus Christ. Someone to relate to when you are in deep, deep, deep trouble.

If you only knew how important these things are.

Feeling uneasy again.

Fast-forward to your deathbed. You're saying good-bye to friends and loved ones. Is there anything you've left unsaid that you'd like to say while you still have the chance?

Who would you like me to look up for you when I get to heaven? Or hell. What would you like me to say to them?

Which of your possessions would you hope will not be thrown out?

I was thinking if I had a bonfire and lost everything, would I care? No. I'm redoing my apartment now and I'm throwing everything out. It was the apartment of a writer, but now I need to make it the apartment of a filmmaker. No clutter. I'm packing up everything for Alan, everything except my eagle paintings, pictures of my family, my birth certificate, divorce papers, I'm keeping all of Leni's stuff, her Purple Heart, a painting of my wife, and a sculpture of her head that I keep in my studio. She was my life for twenty years and it's good to see her.

What would you like to experience one last time?

I'd like to pilot a Stearman biplane or a P51 Mustang. It's the two-thousand-horsepower engine. Little moves get a big reaction. It's so quick on you, you black out. You have to be real young and in good shape to pilot them. They do four hundred and sixty miles per hour in a dive, three hundred at cruising speed. They were built to do the job.

Looking back on it all, what will you miss the most?

Getting good and soused. I'll miss good nights of boozing with the gang, getting drunk as skunks on rum, scotch—single malt—or gin.

Was it worth it? Why?

I didn't make any big, bad errors. I didn't lose a limb, or smoke too much and get cancer. My favorite part? Sitting with another person and we're relating one on one, physically, emotionally, spiritually.

A good artist knows how to download everything, how to absorb everything around them. During my divorce I had a cat named Smoke. I downloaded Smoke and he downloaded me. We both went out of body and floated upstairs. It was frightening, though, so we both went back. I shot back in. I was in a state. If I was in a plane and it was going to crash, I'd go out. The death process, it's the final out-of-body. The only place to go is into the pit, the vacuum, where there's nothing, then that's it.

Everything, even the bad stuff, was exciting. So yeah, it was worth it. Hell yeah. Still is.

Like Sue Rosen and Tolstoy, Rick said something that made me immediately try to distance my life from the truth of his words. *This doesn't apply to me,* I insisted to myself when he said, "You are in charge of what you are, have been, and will be, and if you do not accept this, you will become everything you do not want to become. . . . You'll have a life without people, places, friends . . ." I accept it. I have seen the shadows of what will be. I don't want to become a sterile flower like Sonya, but, okay, now what? I'll do anything, but I don't know what to do.

poLL

MY FANTASY LIFE IS FAIRLY CONSTANT. If I have a piece of time when I have nothing pressing to think about, I daydream. I appreciate reminders that I am not the only one.

The *London Daily Telegraph* reported in January that Syrian Gen. Mustafa Tlass told his men not to attack Italian peacekeeping soldiers during the 1983 chaos in Beirut only because he had a lifelong obsession with the Italian actress Gina Lollobrigida. Gen. Tlass told his men they could "do whatever you want with the U.S., British, and other forces, but . . . I do not want a single tear falling from the eyes of Gina Lollobrigida."

From a poll of 126 people on Echo:

How often do you fantasize during the day? Do you have recurring fantasies?

Six percent said rarely.
Twenty-four percent said one to twelve times a day.
Twenty-six percent said more than a dozen times a day or often.
Fifteen percent said always, constantly, or hundreds of times a day.
Fifty-seven percent said their fantasies were recurring.

My fantasies have changed over time. When I was growing up, I loved to imagine I was suffering from amnesia. It was the ultimate do-over. Now, instead of wiping the slate clean, I fantasize about escape. If I'm going over a bridge, I plan how I would survive should the car, train, or bus I'm in go flying off the side. (Get close to a window that opens, open it, hold on to the luggage rack—if it's a train or a bus—and get out the window and swim away as fast as possible. Don't stop to take off your clothes to make swimming easier until you are confident you are no longer in danger of being sucked under by the sinking car, train, or bus. This is all dependent on whether or not I survive the fall, of course, which is not a certainty, but it's my fantasy, and in my fantasies I always survive.)

Or I fantasize about how I would rebuild civilization in the event of a nuclear war or should aliens destroy New York City. I've also got a rather elaborate daydream about an MIT experiment that involves the world as we know it—reality, everything—going right out the window and my being able to cope with a completely unrecognizable universe. Because I think I am uniquely qualified to do that. I get around the reality constraints by giving the scientists at MIT credit for some pretty amazing advances in their fields. It's laughable, but I enjoy it.

It calms my nothing-lasts, everything-changes, we're-all-going-to-die fears.

But my favorite fantasies involve doing something heroic. For example, if I date a guy with a kid, this triggers my rescuing-my-boyfriend's-child-from-the-subway-tracks fantasy, which goes like this: The kid has fallen onto the subway tracks. There's no time to get the child or grab him and pull him up. I only have enough time to jump down there and push the kid flat in the center of the track and let the train run safely over us. (Note to self: Make sure that's true. Maybe it's better to huddle under the overhang that runs along the platform?)

work

IT'S TOO BAD I WAITED as long as I did. Now I don't have the time to be fussy about who buys Echo and for how much. Here's the problem. I didn't start Echo to get rich. I started Echo because I was unhappy. I was living an awful life and I wanted a better one. That was my business plan: be not-depressed. Not caring about money, however, is a problem when you're an entrepreneur. It's pretty much the key element of a successful business: making money. I wasn't thinking about money. I was thinking about finding people to talk to about David Lynch and Buffy the Vampire Slayer. I managed to keep Echo going for a long time by thinking about money just enough to get by, but long-overdue upgrades caught up with me. Another of my serious business-skills drawbacks—I can't ask for money. Unless you're independently wealthy, your business has to raise capital. But me? Raising money fills me with shame. I've tried every way of getting around it. I've made endless patches to the Echo hardware and software and relied on volunteer help, but time was up. When two companies started talking to me about buying Echo, I listened, because the phone company was sending threatening letters and it was time to admit that maybe, *maybe* I had an idea or two about what works in cyberspace, but I wasn't necessarily the right person to, for instance, negotiate contracts with vendors. (The money thing.) Plus there's that television life I longed to live. My youth was over and it was time to get on with my midlife.

When I met with these two companies—Company A and Company B—the phone company was within days of cutting us off. I loved the people at Company A. They were smart and they understood a lot about the new-media industry. But their service was all about sex. That was great, but I didn't really see where Echo would fit in. The Echo version of an online sex service would be a place where you obsessed endlessly about:

- whether you are doing it right
- what everyone else is doing and why

and

- what medications they're taking for it

Company B, however, had someone who used to work for me and I knew she understood the eccentric heart of Echo. On Echo she calls herself "Miss Outer Boro 1991." Miss Outer Boro 1991 went on to create an odd but appealing world of her own. It was a perfect fit. So I said to her, "Please buy us. Please." She agreed about the fit and she sold the owner of Company B on the idea.

I put the phone company off for two weeks and started

going back and forth with the owner of Company B about the selling price. Sheer agony. Two weeks went by. Me and Company B were getting closer to an agreement but we weren't there yet. I ended up having to do what I hate more than anything else in the world: ask someone for money. I borrowed from my mother, but the money only got me two more weeks. Company B's owner and I got closer. Now I was begging the phone company: "Someone is buying us. I will be able to pay everything I owe you. And you will continue to get money from us because my company is going to turn around." I knew—how many times have they heard that one before?—but I continued. "Please ride out this crisis with us. If you turn off those phone lines you will never collect another dime." They told me that when I declared bankruptcy and our assets were liquidated they would get in line just like everyone else. I remembered when this phone company was just starting out. I was just starting out myself, in the telecommunications department of a company that managed the very large telecommunications services of their clients. The phone company was struggling and desperate for our account. We decided to give them a shot. We liked the idea of giving the little guy a chance. Now I'm the little guy and they're the big guy. *Well,* I thought, to console myself, *my only assets are people and you can't sell them off. If they cut me off, the phone company really won't see another dime, the big meanies.*

Company B made an offer, which I accepted just as the phone company was saying, "That's it, we want our money and we want it now." But just because we'd reached an agreement didn't mean I was going to get a check tomorrow. I didn't want to ask Company B for help. They knew our situation. I figured I'd better come clean so they knew exactly what they were buying, but I didn't think calling them to say "Send the check *now*" was the proper way to begin our new relationship. I headed into full-speed-ahead torture, calling everyone I could think of. I discovered one by-product of not caring about money: poor friends. I kept trying. There are always miracles. As Miss Outer Boro 1991 was fond of saying, "Here's where wishful thinking and denial come in." No go. I couldn't find any money anywhere. I had no choice. I called Miss Outer Boro 1991. "Could you ask Company B's owner for a loan against the purchase price of Echo, to pay the phone company?" She did. Company B wired the money to Echo's bank the next day.

For the first time in a long time the low-level dread that used to run beneath my mornings, noons, and nights was gone. Everything was going to be okay. For a while. I started writing an outline for the TV show I'd like to do. Two shows, actually. It's that computer thing. Always have a backup plan. But I had no idea what a TV show proposal was supposed to look like. I bought books about it, except they're like the books I bought for writing a business plan. The authors should have bought books about how to write how-to books. I couldn't get through them. I talked to a few people and everyone I talked to told me something different. Writing TV shows is like everything else: no one really knows. You're either copying what someone else has done or doing something no one else has done before, so the books aren't going to do you much good. I decided I'd do what I did with Echo. Copy the parts I liked and make up the rest. (When I started Echo, you will remember, I copied the parts I liked from The WELL.) I sent Betsy, my agent, the first drafts and she sent them back with instructions for improvements. I worked on draft two. My lawyers and Company B's lawyers started going back and forth about the contract. That reminded me, I had to find out whose job it was to raise money to make TV shows. So I could make sure I didn't somehow end up with that job. Like anyone would ever give me that job.

fAMiLY

I FOUND MY MISSING and forgotten Civil War veteran ancestor, James Lynch. He died of consumption in his home at 70 Branch Avenue in Providence, Rhode Island, on September 4, 1878, at age forty-two, less than a year after the birth of his eighth child, John Patrick. *Great,* I thought, *forty-two.* When my mother turned fifty my brother Douglas raised his glass and thanked her for making it to fifty. After so many in our family had died in their forties, we finally had reason to hope. I went to a map site on the Internet to see where James died. Number 70 Branch Avenue sits at the southern end of a graveyard. His wife, the former Ellen Smith, died at 110 Ellery Street in Brooklyn. I looked that address up. Also not the happiest place in the world to die, but at least she made it to sixty-three.

Thirteen years after James died, Ellen filed for the pension due her as the widow of a Civil War veteran. An affidavit states that she owned no property and had no other means of support beyond her own labor. My great-great-grandmother was illiterate. She signed all the forms with X's, so I have to figure she wasn't making a lot by her own labor, whatever it was. She had to hire a law firm to help her fill out six forms and supply four certificates so she could get her sad little monthly pension of $10, which would be worth about $177.13 today. That means she probably died poor and struggling. Her friends and neighbors John Mulligan and Peter Feeley signed an affidavit stating that she had never remarried. This means that yet another of my relatives lived alone, without the man of her dreams, until she died, which happened to be the same year that her daughter Jennie gave birth to Jennie's only child, Daisy Armstrong, my grandmother, who also lived without the man of her dreams until the day she died, and whose picture hangs next to me now.

But at least Ellen had the man of her dreams for a while. James was twenty-two when they married, Ellen nineteen. They eventually had eight living children, according to the pension records, though she had given birth to ten. Four years after they were married, in the summer of 1861, James enlisted on a ship called the *Ohio*. He was honorably discharged the following June from the U.S.S. *Connecticut* with the rank of ordinary seaman. Ellen was living at 540 Flushing Avenue in Brooklyn when her first pension check arrived.

My friend Ruby took me there a couple of weeks ago. I brought a camera. I had wanted to see the actual building and the actual front door that Ellen went in and out of every day, but there are projects in its place now. There's not much of a neighborhood left at all. There are old pieces scattered between the industrial sites that have now taken over, and some trees I couldn't identify because it's November and there are no leaves, and a few old buildings with stoops where people would once have sat, gossiping about the neighbors. But mostly it's the kind of place where people work all day, unhappily. I can imagine that in the 1870s it was a sturdy, tight-knit community, poor but proud. A place to come home to, where you felt safe. Back then Ellen had tons of neighbors. Although one of them is closed now, there were two public schools within blocks of each other, and a Catholic school a few blocks away. Once there were enough children to support three schools. The streets must have been wonderfully noisy.

Then we drove to 110 Ellery Street, where Ellen died of pneumonia on June 27, 1904. I have no idea who lived there or who took her in. I just have an address on a death certificate, which says that on June 27, 1904, 110 Ellery Street was a tenement building and that Ellen lived there for four weeks before dying. When we turned the corner we saw a couple of old buildings. There was a chance that the original building was still standing. Ruby's a friend. She wanted me to find what I was looking for. She parked the car and we got out and walked: 104, old building; 106, old building; 108, old building; 110— new projects. I never took out my camera, and now I regret it. The street Ellen Smith Lynch walked on is still there, and it will always be where she died. I have a connection to this spot. I know I will never be back. I should have taken a picture.

I wish these connections were visible. Ellen's daughter lived with her daughter and her granddaughter, my mother, in Sheepshead Bay, and my mother didn't even know Ellen's name, much less her address on the other side of Brooklyn. My friend Jackie took me to my mother's childhood home in Sheepshead Bay just before Halloween. This neighborhood had remained more intact. There were more trees; there were cardboard pumpkins, and black cats and witches, and an unbroken line of cars was parked on every single street. On the streets near Ellen's home in Williamsburg, not far from the old

Navy Yard, groups of cars were parked here and there, looking huddled and alone. This time I got to see the actual building and the actual door, and this time I took a picture.

Every generation so quickly forgets the homes of the last. It's heartbreaking how quickly family is lost. Think about it. Chances are your children's grandchildren won't even know your name, let alone what you did with your life. They will forget about the house where you lived. Maybe that's the way it should be. The meaning I seek is only in my heart, and exists only because I want it to exist. I want a path between the isolated pockets of my family's history. I want a shadowy trail, like a string of phantom Christmas lights running all through Brooklyn, marking every spot and keeping the connection between the past and the present alive. They would be my own private night-lights and they would make me feel safe.

I joined a group called the Daughters of Union Veterans of the Civil War (DUVCW). Jennie and Daisy, my great-grandmother and grandmother, were members. Unfortunately, their tent, Tent 37—chapters are called tents—no longer exists. What almost made up for this was that DUVCW manager Shirley Perry sent me Daisy's original application (she couldn't locate Jennie's). I wondered whether it was in Daisy's handwriting. She was twenty-six years old when she joined. Her initiation fee and badge cost her two dollars. Mine cost twenty-six dollars and came with a small American flag.

In the process of tracking down James and Ellen, I had found twenty-one second cousins once removed who gave birth to more kids than I could count. What would these children be to me? Third cousins? Second cousins twice removed? I'd had some idea that my mother had a few cousins, but she hadn't talked to any of them for years and I'd simply forgotten they existed. They are all the grandchildren of Rose Anna Lynch, one of James and Ellen's children, who married Thomas Craven.

I saw a David Lynch film called *The Straight Story*. (When I started to unravel my past, I was hoping that I would turn out to be related to David Lynch. And to Wes Craven.) I used to think David Lynch and I were two of a kind, but in this film he seems to be suggesting that nothing is stronger than family. Maybe that's true for some, but in my experience there's nothing more fragile. Given the number of people who died alone and are buried on Hart Island, and considering all these ashes sitting forgotten in storage rooms, I'd say I'm closer to being right than David Lynch is. Except there are these twenty-one second cousins (once removed) who appeared out of nowhere and who now call, e-mail, and write. My favorite is Rosemary McCoy, who loves to trace dead relatives, too, and who told me that Ellen Lynch is buried in Calvary Cemetery. (To this day we've been unable to locate James's grave.)

I visited Ellen's grave on a freezing cold day. I had to wait forever for a bus because in that particular spot in Queens few people seem to be going anywhere often. Either that or they all have cars. There were two people listed on the stone in addition to my great-great-grandmother: James H. Lynch, who wasn't the right age to be her husband, so I'm guessing he was her son, and Annie Lynch, whose date of death wasn't listed. All it says is "Annie Lynch. Who died young." I wrote to Calvary Cemetery, requesting an internment list, and along with the list they sent a bill totaling $1,608 for "perpetual care." It must be hard to collect on older graves. I called them to say I had no money. They were understanding. According to the list, eight people are buried in Ellen Lynch's grave: four Lynches, two Moores, one Colligan, and one Craven. The people at Calvary told me that my guess about smushing people down to fit more bodies was correct, "although we would not have chosen the word 'smush.' We bury the first person nine feet down. Then the boxes collapse and we bury more people on top."

The ground in the grave right behind Ellen's was sunken

because someone had been added recently. Two graves farther down was a great big empty hole, waiting for someone else. I noticed that new graves featured photographs of the dead mounted in the stone. There's something disturbing about this practice. This is not what they look like now. I don't know why that should matter, and I can certainly understand wanting to remember them as they were and not how they are at the moment, but the pictures make me even more aware of the fact that they no longer look like that. It's all I can think about. They feel even more dead.

I went inside the chapel at the top of the hill. Two fake Christmas trees sat on either side of the altar, along with two stands of fake candles and a sign that read, "Offering $1.00. Push button to light candle." Under each tube of red glass was an electric light that fluttered in imitation of a real flame. I didn't leave a dollar because I couldn't find anyplace to leave it, and I didn't push any buttons because somebody had already pushed them all. I was afraid that if I turned one off and on I'd cancel out someone else's prayer.

cats

THEY'RE PUTTING LEXINGTON TO SLEEP TODAY. I overheard
them talking about it at the vet's while I was picking up
cat food. It made my stomach hurt. I don't know who Lexington is; I'm just so over-the-top empathic when it comes to cats.
Even imaginary cats. When I'm at a movie, I can't even bear
to watch a cat being threatened. Blow people to bits, I'm fine,
but do something bad to a cat and I'm haunted by it for the
rest of my life—and that means I'm haunted by something that
didn't even really happen. Lexington's owner was bringing him
in at one o'clock, they said. So he's dead now.

I've imagined Veets's and Beams's death. If I ever have to
face putting them to sleep, I'm ready. I've pictured it many
times. First, I'm going to ask my vet to give me a syringe so
I can do it myself at home. He knows I know how to give injections. If he can't, I'm going to pay whatever it takes to

have him come to my apartment and give them the injections there. I don't want their last moments to be in a place that scares them.

I've got the whole death ritual planned out. On the day they die I'll feed them fish and meat and milk and ice cream. They've been on special diets for so long now, for their last meal they're going to have everything they've done without all this time. Then we'll play for a while. They both like ribbons; Veets likes Ping-Pong balls.

The next part I always go over lovingly because it's the part that's painful but bittersweet. I tell them why I fell in love with them. I go over all their special qualities and traits and my favorite memories. I cry, but it's a good cry. I talk about how I hope those tunnel people are right and that we'll see each other again, but I don't think they are because I read a pretty plausible explanation for those visions—which I've completely forgotten, except it had something to do with brain chemistry— and I can't lie, so I also talk about how lucky we all were to have found each other, since we only live once and only had this one chance.

Then, if it's Beamers, I'll put him on the couch or my desk chair; if it's Veets, I'll put him in a basket or a box, these being their favorite spots. Euthanasia takes two shots. If the vet is giving the shots to Beams, I'm going to ask him to give the shot and then leave immediately. Beams will be so frightened with him there. If it's Veets, the vet doesn't have to run out the door, but he still has to go. I want to say good-bye privately. I wonder if I can get Valium to give them first. (And me too, while we're at it.) If I'm giving the shots, after the first injection I'll kiss the top of their heads about a hundred billion times, then I'll look them in the eye and do the blinking thing that they both like, and then I'll inject them for the second time. Then I'll die inside as I wait and watch. The fantasy stops there because I usually start choking. I'm not entirely sure me giving them the shots is such a good idea.

Also, I've read that the reality may not be as peaceful as I imagine it. Some cats urinate or defecate when you put them to sleep. They may struggle and cry.

Nothing will reduce the devastating effect their deaths will have on me. I know they are only cats. I hate this. I don't have to explain myself to pet owners. Rent *Old Yeller*.

fANtAsY

EVERY EVENING two steady streams of airplanes fly by my win-dow. I can see them when I'm lying on the couch with Veets and Beams. They watch pigeons while I watch planes. Their heads move up and down; mine moves like I'm watching a slow-motion tennis match. I'm hoping that the planes either (A) turn out to be UFOs, or (B) crash. I want to watch a plane fall out of the sky. I mean, not really. I don't want people to die. That's not it. It would just be something to see. I don't know where the urge comes from. What's that? Is it turning? Landing? Oh my God! Then the explosion, bright flash, maybe smoke. Should I go to where it crashed?

I have a book of flight-data recordings from plane crashes. You can read what the pilot and crew said to each other during the last minutes of their lives. They usually don't say anything philosophical. They're not panicking. What they're doing right up until the very end is trying not to crash. They are the ultimate professionals. By the time they realize there's nothing they can do, they have time only for a few last words. Typical final-flight talk goes kind of like this:

"Okay, what are the readings on the *something something*?"
"*Something something.*"
"Did you try the *something something*?"
"Check."
"Sir, I heard about a flight where they pulled it up by inverting the *something something*."
"Johnson, invert the *something something*."
"Inverting."
"Shit."
"Oh shit."
"I love you, Mom."
Tape ends.

It's not enough that I will have to actually endure death someday. I have to give myself anxiety attacks going over the saddest, most hopeless evidence I can find that it's all going to end—always sadly, sometimes horribly.

A few of my time-honored, favorite death stories.

I read in Kenneth Iserson's *Death to Dust* that James H. Bradford is the only person still cryogenically frozen from the first batch of seventeen. He was a retired psychology professor who died and was frozen in 1973. His corpse is still in California. The rest have thawed out, either by accident or by design. I know that they died, that they were never coming back in the first place, that, realistically, cryogenics is a long shot—if it could be considered a shot at all—but even if they never had so much as a slim chance they nonetheless thought they had. There's something immeasurably sad about this. However false the hope, it's an extra and unnecessary disappointment thrown on top of everything else. Quit thawing out frozen people!

Then there are premature-burial stories. The worst one can be found in, again, *Death to Dust*—a great death source—about a little girl who was thought to have died of diphtheria while visiting relatives in South Carolina in the 1850s. Everyone was afraid of catching what she had, so they quickly put her in a local mausoleum instead of taking her body home. Years later, when the family whose mausoleum it was went back in to bury a son killed in the Civil War, they found a small pile of bones near the door. How long did she wait, alone in the dark, before she died? Sometimes, when they move cemeteries, they find bodies twisted around, their hair pulled out, or the inside of the casket torn up by someone's struggle to get out.

Iserson says that undertakers have to take the most care with dead infants and children because parents frequently want to pick them up. They have to make sure that the body stays round and natural-feeling. Adults they let go all flat on the bottom.

I sometimes imagine the final moments of the last czar, Nicholas, and his wife, Alexandra, and their children, Olga, Tatiana, Maria, Anastasia, and Alexis, who were all shot to death. A couple of the girls didn't die from the bullets because they had stuffed their clothes with jewels. The soldiers had to bayonet them to death. Imagine someone going at a child with a bayonet while she screamed and cried and writhed on the floor, surrounded by her dead and dying family. Eighteen bayonet marks were found in the floor in one spot alone. How could someone bayonet a screaming little girl eighteen times?

I imagine my own death. From a heart attack. I feel the walls of my heart seizing up, shutting off all my chances, an immovable, nonnegotiable barrier. My heart feels like it's hard, like a small boulder. I can't talk. I don't know if it's because I really can't or if I'm too caught up in the pain of the heart attack and the shock of dying. *Wait, wait, wait, just give me a second to deal with this. Let me get my bearings and I'll be okay.* The oddest thing about my imagined death is the noise. It's the loudest thing I've ever heard in my life, as if the universe is screaming *"NO!"* at the top of its lungs. I believe I'm no longer really hearing and the noise is all internal. It's the sound of my own blood rushing.

I think of death as an explosion. Some people go off like firecrackers, some like atomic bombs, most like fireflies. I want to be conscious when I die, I've decided. I don't want to miss anything. Especially the last thing. In the novel *Cold Mountain*, one character, who is witnessing the death of another, asks her, "What will ease your passing?" Nothing. Still, it's the last thing to go through, so I would like to be awake for it. It won't be a horrible memory because I won't be alive to remember it. Or regret my decision.

Why do I work myself into this ridiculous state of panic? There isn't anything I can do about dying. It must be like being sucked out of a window on an airplane that's crashing. You don't want to go flying off into the sky, thousands of feet above the ground, but you don't exactly want to get back on that falling plane either. There's no escape. So what do I get out of it?

I read a book review by Susan Cheever about a guy who helped his wife, who had multiple sclerosis, commit suicide. I'll never forget the point Cheever made at the end of her review. "We like to forget that we are never choosing between life and death, only between death now and death in a little while. But death is inevitable—our shared fate—love is not so inevitable."

That's the reason why I spook myself by imagining that final moment and by recounting all my favorite stories of death: I'm afraid I will waste the second half of my life and not love as much as I can right now, while I still have the chance. I try to stop Daisy and Emma and the Sammises and all the rest from being lost forever to diminish the power of death and to make me remember to live. I may be cannibalizing their moment of glory, but what the hell, it works. I feel better.

The earth is a burial ground. Layer after layer of love and lives lived and forgotten, one on top of another, a constantly churning surface that we smush down, not giving a thought to the endless line of lives who decompose into nothing recognizable beneath us.

What about the lucky people who are remembered in someone's heart? The people who remember them will die. We all disappear. Like all the people packed beneath the earth in Prospect Cemetery, and all the Sammises who have come and gone in Huntington.

In the end, what's left? What happens to our things when our life is over? Not much. The rate of decay is heartlessly swift. A short time after I die all I'll have to show for myself is the debris that may or may not be found by someone who will never know who I was, and who can't know that what might look like trash to them was treasure to me.

ROMANCE

I'VE STOPPED GOING OUT once a week to meet someone. What's the use? It's tiring and, besides, it's not working. Either I'm going to come across the man of my dreams while I go about living what I call my life, or I'm not. These days I'm trying to adapt the Gaia hypothesis to my life. For example, if you pollute a river, rather than trying to clean it or take the poison out, the best thing to do, according to this theory, is just stop poisoning the river (duh) and let nature take its course. The earth is a self-regulating entity. If there's a problem with one part, the environment will correct itself in another. If I leave my man-of-my-dreams problem alone and quit trying to fix it, then slowly, slowly, it will correct itself—as long as I stop doing whatever it is I am doing to "pollute" my "river." Very New Age–y, I know, but it suits my purposes, so shut up. The hard part is identifying where the poison might be coming from. (It always goes back to Sonya. What am I doing to sabotage my chances?)

But I worry that my Gaia Hypothesis of Romance is just a new and fancier form of giving up. As if my ideal man is going to fall into my lap. Or suddenly appear online (as I secretly hope). In fact, I've just noticed that while I teach a course about what people do in cyberspace, I've never covered virtual romance, a huge reason why people go online. Purely for research purposes, of course, I go to Match.Com, the online dating service I keep hearing about on Echo.

I'm asked to fill out a profile about myself and who I'm looking for. I don't say much. I'm only here to explore for my class, after all. "I live for *Buffy the Vampire Slayer*," I say, and when I'm asked to finish the sentence "My friends would describe me as . . ." I write, "An alien life form." I could upload a photograph, but I don't. I pick "Lewton" for my nickname (for the movie director and producer Val Lewton) and within hours I start getting e-mail from men wanting to meet me.

At first I was excited. I couldn't help myself. I checked my e-mail every few minutes. I'd heard the stories. "And just when she had given up on ever finding someone she met him online." Now I understand the appeal. Miraculous, and effortless, love. I went back to Match.Com to see how the men who'd e-mailed me described themselves. Oh, God. The profiles all read as if they were written by the same earnest, humorless, man. A lot of sunsets and sentiments along the lines of "I'm looking for that special lady," who has to be pretty, by the way—even though to judge by their pictures, most of the men weren't catches themselves.

The first e-mail I got was short and unenticing. "Hi. I liked your profile. Please look at mine." The next was from a good-looking fellow TV fanatic with an artistic background, except he tried to use his ex-wife to impress me. (She works in the movies.) The next guy described himself as a "handsome and very boyish 53-year-old." He looked like Truman Capote. A lot of the e-mail I got was little more than lists. "I like hiking, swimming, tennis, and going to the movies and museums." One guy was gorgeous, and he had three photos up there to prove it, but all he could talk about was his height and weight. He even posted his waistline measurements. There were a couple of guys who were not-attractive in a way I happen to find very attractive. They had a kind of a goofy-sweet-smart look, but again, zero personality.

One guy said right off, "I don't own a TV." I don't know why he bothered writing. Another was Republican. Some guys talked about their master's degrees, and wrote me pages and pages from which absolutely nothing stood out. There's something a little disconcerting about people who write so much to a stranger who only gives a few sentences of information about herself.

One of the last e-mail messages I got told me to respond "not interested" if I didn't want to talk to him. "It's the courteous and right thing to do." That creeped me out. The very last e-mail was from the first person to ask me where I got the name "Lewton" from, and was it from Val Lewton? I almost answered him simply because he'd guessed.

But I didn't write anyone back. I don't know how to respond to vulnerability from strangers.

Give up, quit trying, nature will provide the best correction. That's what I'm banking on these days. But there's a problem with my Gaia Hypothesis of Romance. People on Echo point out that "best correction" is a tricky proposition. Nature doesn't care. As far as my river-polluting example goes, nature might well decide that the best thing to do is to eliminate the species putting the chemicals into the water in the first place. Do I really want to put my love life in nature's hands? I'm thinking, *Maybe nature will deliver Ruben Blades right to my doorstep.* But what if nature decides the best guy is one who doesn't own a

TV and is looking for that "special lady"? And then I kill him because I just can't stand it anymore, which is just what nature intended because nature has decided that eliminating the Special Lady/No TV Guy would be best for all concerned, and that what's best for you, missy, is that you remain absolutely and entirely alone.

deAtH

I'D BEEN TRYING FOR MONTHS to find out who the sad person was who lived in my building and might turn out be my ghost. Now, it isn't so much who she was, but which, of all the sad people who have lived in my building, she was. There are so many to choose from. I've uncovered story after story of every-day, unspectacular, quiet misery. I'm naming my building the House of Pain.

The night that Mikal told me my apartment had a ghost, the first thing I did was try to find out who her landlord was. "She lived here in the fifties," Mikal had said. *It's possible that the landlord is still alive and remembers a particularly sad woman,* I thought. I called the current landlord but he was relatively new and he only knew the person he bought the building from. Then I went down to my basement. You have to see my base-ment to understand why I thought that was a good place to begin. It's so unchanged. Some of the rooms still have dirt floors. It smells like old things that have been wet for decades. When I reached for the light—wondering if there *were* any lights down there, which there weren't—I almost expected to be turning on a gas lamp. After going as far as I could with a flashlight, which I waved in front of me so I'd get hit in the arm and not the face by the tarantulas I knew were just waiting to pounce on me, I found a clipboard by the boiler with permits going back to 1973. The owners' names were written in the upper-right-hand corner. I found something else: a nicely typed index card, dated 10/16/73, with instructions about where to place the permit, signed by a Miss Star. I found the "Miss" touching. Miss Star. Miss Horn. I miss "Miss." Did Miss Star live in my apartment? Is she the one haunting me? She could have been living there since the fifties. I wrote down all the names.

Then I went to the Municipal Archives. It's amazing what you can find out about your building. Mine was built in 1894 by Joseph Mandelbaum on farmland once owned by Abigail Hammond. After Mandelbaum, ownership passed to Lee Dressner, and then to Daniel Farrell, to Edward and Dorothy Faruola, and to Mary D. Sheffield in 1946. Sheffield owned the building until 1963, so she was the landlord when my ghost was living here. But what did this get me? How was I going to track down Mary Sheffield? I called every Mary and M. Sheffield in New York and in Florida, the place where people from New York generally retire, but none of them turned out to be my Perry Street ghost landlord.

Next I went to the library. After explaining how to get the reverse phone directories and the 1905, 1915, and 1925 census records, the librarian asked me why I was trying to find out who'd lived in my building. I didn't want to tell him I was looking for a ghost, so I said only it was for a book I was writing. Then he said, "Because I was going to ask you if you were

210

looking for a ghost." A lot of people in New York are haunted, it turns out.

The 1905 census records turned up a lot of potentially unhappy people. In apartments the size of the one where I now live alone lived families with five or ten people or more—children, in-laws, nieces, and nephews—and with heads of households making their living as laborers, janitresses, and dry-goods salesmen. John and Josephine Marlia lived in my building with their six children, but the census records indicated that Josephine had given birth to ten. Did the other four die? Or grow up and move out? And when did she start having those kids? She was only thirty-one by the time she gave birth to the tenth. John was a "stendon" on a riverboat, whatever that is. There were a couple of widowers living with their children. Mary Griffen, thirty-six, lived with her five daughters, two of whom worked as salesgirls, and had one boarder, Michael Galvin, thirty, who was a bartender. I immediately hoped that Michael and Mary had a thing. Although it was possible that one of these children continued to live here until the fifties and became my ghost, it seemed unlikely.

The 1925 census was less sad, if only because people were having fewer kids and had a little more room. Occupations like "lineman" and "telephone operator" are showing up along with "tinsmith" and "longshoreman." Nothing jumped out at me, though. Plus, neither census gave apartment numbers. There's no way of knowing which of these people lived in my apartment. On to the phone books.

I went through the directories for the fifties, but like the census, there was no way of knowing who lived in which apartment. I saw that my neighbor Peter Tessa was living here in the fifties. He died in the early eighties, a few years after I moved in. He was dead a week before they found him. When I asked the police crowded outside his apartment what had happened, one of them replied, "Don't you smell it?" I hadn't.

A couple of weeks later the door to his apartment was open. It looked as if the place hadn't been renovated or repainted for a hundred years. Instead of a refrigerator there was an ice-box. An engineer's report that was completed not long after he died read: "This entire apartment is a violation. It is a violation of a man's right to a decent living space within an urban environment purporting to support and defend the less affluent but self-supporting members of society after their productive working years. The pervasive and defined neglect is an insult to the dignity of the now deceased occupant. It represents the essence of a forgotten soul who left this earth without the final knowledge of a clean and decent home. . . ." I found Tessa's high school yearbook sitting on the floor. There were all sorts of nice predictions for him under his picture. "Will die alone and only be discovered because of the smell" was not among them.

I spent months trying to get permission to go through police archives, to see if any crimes were reported for my building in the fifties, only to discover that they didn't save much and that what little they had was not sorted by building. "No, we won't let you go through everything in order to find something we may or may not have for your building." It was a bit startling to learn how little the police saved. "What about the old precinct log books?" Thrown out. "What about evidence in older crimes?" Thrown out. "What if the case is reopened?" Silence. They suggested I go back to the Municipal Archives. Old court records list the name and address of the defendant and plaintiff for each case. I went through everything. I was faked out twice. I saw "Perry Street" and thought *Aha!* but both mentions turned out to involve different buildings. I did learn that at the turn of the century people were picked up a lot more often for cruelty to animals than they are now, and that if someone was picked up for vagrancy it was most likely a woman.

It all comes down to Lotte Faderwick. Lotte is eighty-eight years old and she lives in a nursing home three blocks from my building, where she lived for sixty-five years. We always said hello to each other in the halls. I hope she remembers me. More important, I hope she remembers the people she said hello to in the halls in the 1950s. The name "E. Conway" is on an old nameplate right outside my door. Maybe Lotte will know who E. Conway was. None of the census records or phone books showed a Conway.

I arrived at the nursing home feeling a little anxious. I told them I wanted to visit Lotte, and everyone was glad I was visiting, but I made them ask her first to see if it was okay. I thought she might not remember me and might not want a visit from a stranger. "Come on up," she said. I never would have recognized her if someone hadn't pointed her out. She didn't recognize me, either. In fact, she thought I was someone else at first, and I corrected her, but she didn't care. We had a nice visit. I go back every couple of weeks. Every time I say, "Good-bye, I'll see you next week," she smiles and answers, "If I'm still here." Lotte is easy to talk to. While telling me stories, she periodically grabs her walker, struggles to get up, then sits back down again. "For exercise," she explains. She moved to Perry Street sometime in the 1920s—she no longer knows exactly when—with her husband Edward, who died in 1979. Lotte's memories are inconsistent. Her stories are composites—the details never change, but they get shuffled around. One week, an alcoholic named Laura lived in my apartment; the next week, Laura lived in the apartment below me and maybe her name wasn't Laura. What is consistent is the unhappiness. We may not know which tenant was always wandering in the halls or sitting on the stairs, crying, but there was always some woman who was afraid to go home because her husband was a drunk and sometimes he'd smash her in the face. Someone else was evicted because she couldn't pay the rent and she offered herself to every man in the building if in exchange he would take her in.

During one visit I showed Lotte the list of names I'd gathered from the phone books. She went through them.

Evicted.

Evicted.

Got sick and died.

Drank.

Her husband drank.

Would push you down the stairs if she thought she could get away with it.

Died.

She knew the Miss Star who neatly typed the instructions for the boiler permit. Miss Star lived here in the fifties, and she lived alone, Lotte told me. She worked for the phone company, but she was always ill. She went into the hospital one day and no one ever saw her again. An excellent ghost candidate, except she lived on the first floor. "What about E. Conway?" I asked. Lotte told me there were two tenants named Conway: a husband and wife who lived above her, and a single woman who lived alone in my apartment. The wife who lived above Lottie had a bladder problem. She peed wherever she went. She also eventually went into the hospital and was never seen again. And her husband was another one who died and wasn't found until the halls and apartments started filling up with flies, which came into Lotte's living room through the window over the fire escape. Lotte couldn't remember the first name of the Conway who lived in my apartment, but she remembers that she lost her job and my apartment. She's a possibility. Such sad lives. I'm starting to wonder why ghosts aren't meaner. Mikal tells me they are. "But your ghost loves you. You're lucky."

I told him Lotte's stories. "Your ghost is sad," he said once again. "I feel for it." "I just put up Christmas lights for us," I told him. "I've got fresh water out for her, and a pumpkin and now Christmas lights. Do you think she feels better now?"

"The ghost realizes you're trying to make up for letting all those people come in there and move things around." (I had people in to paint the place.) "Your ghost loves you. It feels protective of you. It feels better the more it sees you. Of course, that might not be the best thing for you."

"Why not?"

"Because, Stacy, you won't get out much."

It's true. I'm going to be another in a long line of women in my building who live and die in the House of Pain.

How many people live sad lives and die without protest? There were hundreds and hundreds of people in the short history of my one small building alone. It's like Joe's mother says: "Everyone has the same dreams." Everyone in the House of Pain wanted to be someone special. No one wanted to die and not be found until they smelled or filled their neighbors' living rooms with death flies. It's not just my building, it's a world of pain. There are too many people who have good reasons to stay behind and haunt the world that disappointed them. I could very well become one of them. I'm bound to be disappointed. I'm not sure I want to haunt Perry Street. Unless, of course, Veets and Beams can haunt it with me.

cats

Veterinarians are doctors who eventually see all their patients die. Pretty quickly, too. City cats, who live longer than cats in the country, generally only make it to fifteen. So veterinarians not only watch every one of their patients die, they watch their patients' children live and die and then their children's children. People doctors, at least some of the time, get to treat their patients, then watch them go on and live long lives, and never witness their ends. Every time I take my cats to the Cat Practice, I think, *This is what I want to do with my twilight years. Work at the Cat Practice.* But could I watch cat after cat after cat, all my little patients, die?

I talked to Dr. William "Skip" Sullivan. Dr. Sullivan has taken care of Veets and Beams almost from the beginning. He's the one who told me I had to calm down because my anxiety was freaking them out. He's the one who tried to be sympathetic when informing me that I now had two diabetic cats. The last time I was there, when he leaned in to check Veets's heartbeat, he kissed the top of Veets's head as if this were the most natural thing in the world to do.

Dr. Sullivan was led to the irresistibleness of my cat's head by his experiences during the Vietnam War. He was twenty-three, an infantryman, and what he saw in Vietnam was so awful, he had to do something as far from it as he possibly could. He once watched a Navy man save a Marine by whipping out a scalpel and executing a perfect tracheotomy in fifteen seconds, so he thought, *Something to do with healing.* He considered treating people, then decided he would rather take care of cats. His current patient load numbers roughly four thousand. That's four thousand tiny heartbreaks in store for Dr. Sullivan. In another fifteen years there will be thousands and thousands more. I'm not sure I could take it. Dr. Sullivan said at first it was unbearable for him, and that he's had to learn to distance himself a little—but not too much.

I don't think he needs to worry. The man kisses cats. And the look on his face when he told me the story of Rogue. Rogue was an eight-year-old gray-and-white that belonged to one of his employees. He was torn to pieces by two pit bulls. The shock, all the blood he lost—he was a mess. Dr. Sullivan spent four and a half hours in surgery, removing Rogue's spleen and the crushed part of his intestines and fixing a hole in his bladder. The employee kept asking him to put Rogue to sleep, but Dr. Sullivan thought there was a chance. Sullivan thought Rogue was getting better. The employee insisted that he was not. On the second day after surgery Rogue experienced what Dr. Sullivan calls lift-off. He rallied. For a few hours he really started coming around. Then he died that night. Dr. Sullivan tells me doctors and nurses have since told him that dying people sometimes experience the same thing: they lift off before crashing. Twenty years later Dr. Sullivan still feels doubly bad because, one, Rogue died, and two, he insisted on trying to do something after the owner had asked him to stop. He looked at all the vital signs and they told him Rogue had a chance. But Rogue's owner saw signs Dr. Sullivan didn't.

He's haunted by Rogue's memory. You can see it in the way he moves in his chair when he talks about him. I'd be haunted, too. My apartment would be packed with little cat ghosts, forever coming around the corners, an endless, continuous line of them. What do most cats die of? Kidney disease. Of course, that's one of the things Beamers has. That's what the drip is for. "How long do cats live once they're diagnosed with kidney disease?" I ask, trying to look calm. "Four or five years would be a spectacular run for a cat with kidney disease," he says. "So Beamers has maybe two years to live," I say in a voice about an octave higher. "No, no, no, you never know," Dr. Sullivan replies. I know you never know, but not only is it amazing that Beamers is still alive, Dr. Sullivan's just admitted it would be "spectacular" if he lived two more years. I want to reassure Dr. Sullivan. "He's a spectacular cat," I tell him.

"Who's the meanest cat you ever treated?" I ask Dr. Sullivan. "Franz Joseph," he tells me. Franz Joseph regularly mauled his owners, Dr. Sullivan, and Dr. Sullivan's technicians. The owners kept him, he says, because they had rescued him and were loving people. Things got better when Dr. Sullivan put Franz Joseph on antiseizure medicine.

One of Dr. Sullivan's favorite cats was a thirty-inch-long, twenty-two-pound cat named Mississippi. "He was the biggest cat I ever treated who wasn't overweight. He was all black, like a small panther." He calls Mississippi one of his "gentle giants." Mississippi's owners lived on the first floor of a building in Stuyvesant Town and they'd let him out to walk around the grounds. Dr. Sullivan said he moved through the bushes as if he were stalking animals or small children.

Who was the most depressed cat? He knew a pair of Siamese

cats, male and female, who were together their whole lives. The female died when she was fourteen, and the male almost followed her. "Most cats live more day to day," he says, and "handle the death of another cat, even cats they are close to, relatively well. Siamese cats form stronger bonds with people and other cats." This cat wouldn't eat—he was absolutely lifeless—even though every test proved that physically he was fine. "He was dying of grief." Dr. Sullivan finally suggested the owners get a kitten, and they did. The cat got better.

Which immediately brings the conversation back to Veets and Beams. "Should I get a kitten for Veets when Beamers dies?" I ask. I'm convinced Beamers will go first, and they're so close. "Will Veets be lonely?" His answer? "Wait and see. Not all cats react like that. Veets might be okay."

Cat remains are usually cremated. The container is different from the one for people. It's made of tin, about the size of a small paint can, and covered with flowers. A small artificial flower is attached to the lid. The crematory has urns, but Dr. Sullivan thinks the quality is substandard and he doesn't recommend them. The remains are then either scattered in Long Island Sound or returned to the owners. About half the owners want the remains back.

What about the owners? The worst are the ones who want to have their cats put to sleep because they claw the furniture or "we're moving." Dr. Sullivan won't euthanize a cat for those reasons. I've spent a lot of time at the Cat Practice. I was there when one owner was told to give her cats pills and she asked them to put the cat to sleep instead. They explained to her that the cat's illness was not terminal and that he'd be fine after taking these pills. She explained that that wasn't the point. She didn't want to have to give her cat pills. "We won't put down an essentially healthy cat." "I don't want to have to give my cat pills." Standoff. Everyone in the waiting room bonded in hatred of her. *Save him! Save him!* I begged in my head. No

219

one wanted Dr. Sullivan to return the cat to her. *Save him!* She stormed out without the cat, thank God. Dr. Sullivan has to put about 150 cats to sleep a year, and he will only euthanize cats with irreversible diseases who are suffering.

The oddest owner he ever met had MPD (multiple personality disorder). He'd tell one personality to bring the cat in or give the cat pills, and another personality would insist that he'd never spoken with her. Dr. Sullivan has met three of her personalities—one perfectly nice, one hostile, and one not very bright. He says if she weren't so nice he wouldn't have her as a client. Does he ever refuse clients? Yes. Clients who are abusive to the people who work for him are sent letters and copies of their cat's records and told they may never come back.

Could I learn to withstand the endless procession of dead cats without turning into a sleepless, tortured wreck? Could I ever work at the Cat Practice? "Do I have to get some sort of degree?" I ask Dr. Sullivan. I'm hoping the answer is no, so that I can continue to fantasize about working at the Cat Practice someday. If he says yes, that kills the reality requirement, because I know I'll never go back to school.

"No," he answers. "I'll hire someone if they're willing to start at the bottom, cleaning cat cages." I'm willing. Plan G.

deATH

Ever since Hart Island became a potter's field, practically
every article about the place has described it as having gray,
overcast skies, wheeling gulls, and barren fields. If an image
was grim and desolate it was used. There was a brief moment
when the island was described as "fertile," back when the city
first bought it, intending to build an industrial school for des-
titute boys, but the minute they buried Louisa Van Slyke—a
twenty-four-year-old who died alone at Charity Hospital in
1869, and that's all I can find out about her—no one mentions
that the sun shines as spectacularly on Hart Island as it does
everywhere else. Or that the sound of the water and the constant wind that whips up bright whitecaps on every wave between here and City Island make you feel more absolutely,
undeniably, thrillingly alive, while you walk down abandoned

roads past decaying houses, theaters, and dormitories, than you do in the middle of Manhattan's furious and frantic bustle.

If I were going to be buried—and I don't want to be—I'd rather be buried there than in any other cemetery, where it's nothing but dead, dead, dead, in a scary, unnatural way. Hart Island is peaceful and stimulating at the same time. *I can't wait to tell Sue Rosen,* I thought right away. *It's going to be okay.*

In addition to being the site of a workhouse for boys and a potter's field, over the years Hart Island has also been the site of a hospital for yellow fever, an insane asylum, a homeless shelter, various prisons, alcohol and drug rehabilitation programs, and a Nike missile base.

Solomon Riley seems to have been one of the few people to see Hart Island as I see it. He bought four acres on the southeastern end of the island for $35,000 in 1923 when the city, which had been offered the opportunity to purchase it, decided to pass. Two years later he announced that he would open a "Negro Coney Island," and proceeded to build a boardwalk, a dancehall, eight cottages, and a bathing pavilion made out of an old iceboat. But the city wouldn't grant his company, Spectacle Realty, a license to run a park. They gave various reasons. The presence of a park might make it easier for the prisoners to smuggle contraband. Or escape. Officials swore that racial prejudice had nothing to do with it. Solomon kept building. The following year, the city took possession of the site in condemnation proceedings. In response, the Supreme Court awarded Solomon and Elizabeth Riley $144,015 in 1927 for the buildings and the land. The city's experts had estimated they were worth $87,144. Supreme Court Justice Peter J. Hatting estimated differently. Later, there were memos and meetings to ask just whose bright idea it was to decline the purchase in 1923 anyway, when they could have had it for a song. The mayor's name came up. If anything ever came of the matter, it was kept behind closed doors.

Melinda Hunt's an artist who did a book on Hart Island. I called her because I had read that she helped people find friends and relatives buried there. I thought I could help her by creating a Web site. Melinda's the one who gave me 130 years' worth of articles about the island. Her book, and the photographs by her partner Joel Sternfeld, confirmed what I'd always suspected: Hart Island is not as creepy as 130 years' worth of articles would have you believe. Melinda Hunt is like the wind off the Long Island Sound—when you're with her you wake up. We had both wanted to get to Hart Island. She made it, and I didn't. Thank God she took me with her the next time she went. Otherwise I might never have gotten there. I took my old Brownie Hawkeye camera and was determined to get the shot of my dreams, because this would probably be my one and only chance.

The friendless Louisa Van Slyke was buried on Hart Island on April 20, 1869. Since then she has been joined by around 750,000 others. I went through the records at the Municipal Archives. They keep the historical ones. The Department of Corrections (which runs the island) keeps the current records, and right on the island itself. First I checked 1956, the year I was born. The records for the adults buried that year are lost, unfortunately; all that's left are the records for the babies. Eighteen babies born on my birthday, June 3, are buried on Hart Island. They were all picked up at city hospitals except one, an "unknown colored female" who was picked up on 140th Street and Harlem River. Two sets of twins are among the June 3 dead. They are identified as Krenzel (A) and Krenzel (B), who lived a day, and Hathaway (A), who also lived a day, and Hathaway (B), who made it to two. I found later records for a Kazar (A) and a Kazar (C), which I hope means that Kazar (B) survived. I checked the remaining records and no Kazar (B) appears, but the records are incomplete. *Please don't be among the missing records, Kazar (B).*

The causes of death for the June 3 babies, and all the babies buried that year, are listed as confidential. The amount of information in the records varies from year to year. A frequent cause of infant death in earlier records is "marasmus." I look the word up. Etymology: "LL [Late Latin], from Greek *marasmos*, fr. *marainein*, to waste away . . . a condition of chronic undernourishment occurring esp. in children and usu. caused by a diet deficient in calories and proteins." Common causes of death among adults: alcoholism, mania, dementia, syphilis, smallpox, suicide, and drowning. Lots of drowning among the Hart Island dead.

Some years list the deceased's religion. A one-year-old child named Mojica, who was picked up from Willowbrook State Hospital and buried the same day as my fellow-birthdate babies, is identified as Catholic. The people in charge of burials would always identify the Catholics if they could because they used to bury the Catholics in a separate piece of consecrated ground. A priest would ride the ferry over to Hart Island twice a week and say Mass. Now they send someone once a year, on Ascension Day, also known as Holy Thursday (the day Christ is said to have ascended into Heaven). The Catholics are the only ones to send anyone at all. (The Grand Army of the Republic used to send a twelve-piece band once a year, on Decoration Day, to commemorate the Union soldiers buried there. But the soldiers' remains were moved to Cypress Hills National Cemetery in 1941.)

The records for 1956 list surnames only, though lists for other decades give the first initial and sometimes the whole name. Heavenly Peace Love, for example, died just after Christmas, on December 28, in 1960, at the age of ninety.

The records also include a separate section for limbs. They list the person's name and cause of death and then identify the limb that was buried. I couldn't figure this section out at all. Is the limb all that was left of the dead person? Or do the records mean that this is the date of the limb's death, and the rest of the person is alive? No body part is too small. There's a full record: name of the owner, where the limb was found, the date of death and date of burial, section number and position, for someone's "left great toe." There are lots of toes buried on Hart Island, it turns out. There are more legs than arms, and in one case only the thigh and not the whole leg, and in one unforgettable case the "lower ext. of body," found on Seventh Avenue and Sterling Plaza in Brooklyn on February 12, 1961, and buried almost four months later, on May 9. When possible, the smallest coffins—baby coffins, actually—are used for limbs.

I couldn't help thinking of the Mormons, who are busy keeping track of every person who was ever born, lived, and died. Are they keeping track of limbs as well? And what do they do in the cases of all the unidentified men, women, children, and "lower ext. of bodies"?

Another thing I couldn't figure out was why a name would be listed twice. At first I thought these must be twins, but there were so many of them, and then I thought the repetition might mean married couples being buried together. Except both people named were always exactly the same age. When I started going through the earlier records, which list the complete name, I found that the paired records were almost always of the same person. So these were neither twins nor partners in death, but two records for the same person. And in every case, the second record indicated that the person was in a separate box. One person was getting two boxes. Why?

The whole time I was on the island I kept thinking, *I have to find Michelle Rosen.* "You will show us the baby trench, won't you?" I asked Captain Eugene Ruppert, the corrections officer who was escorting us. He would. Everyone is buried in trenches, and each trench is given a bright white marker, which stands in the field like a miniature castle. Each marker gives the trench number and date. They keep track of the position of every person inside each trench so they can be disinterred later. The city will disinter bodies, at its own expense, up to nine years after burial. After twenty-five years the trenches are reused. There are 150 adults between every white marker in the windy fields. In the baby field there are a thousand. A gull flew by with a fish in its mouth. I can't help feeling sorry for the fish. *Poor thing, swimming along and swimming along and then fuck! An explosion of incomprehensible changes with no time to think. Rush upward. Bright. New world. Can't breathe. Flying through the air. Tiny heart going a mile a minute. Dying, dying.* Death imminent, either by suffocation or by being eaten alive. This whole indifferent birth, life, death process. I'll never get used to it. I'll never find peace.

"What about the smell?" I ask. It's got to smell sometimes. Captain Ruppert explained that, yes, it used to smell, because the inmates would trudge through the pools of body fluids that collected in the trenches and then, without wiping their boots, they'd walk around inside the buildings in which they lived, worked, and slept. But now they had stricter cleaning processes and didn't wait as long to fill up the trenches.

We headed to the baby trench. The roads on Hart Island are like country lanes. Trees planted on either side grow in and over to form an elegant arch, giving an almost royal feel to our procession past decaying buildings set back among willows, poplars, beech, oak, and maple. "Be right back," I said, running into the woods to get a closer look at every building we pass. Melinda and Ruppert had seen them all before. They stood and talked while I investigated. All the doors were boarded up, but I could see inside through the windows. I walked the length of one long building, looking into window after window, and saw walls painted rose, and blue, and with gold paint flecks, then straight through the glassless windows on the other side to green leaves, blue and white sky, and sun. Wall, window, wall, window: it was like slowly turning the crank of an old nickelodeon.

"It used to be a theater," Ruppert told me when I rejoined them. I wondered, did prisons still have theaters, where inmates performed for each other and the guards? There had been a crude, inmate-produced magazine called *The Hart Islander* for a time. It had a sense of what I can only call innocence. Or hope. The December 25, 1959, issue, which begins, "Our first issue—our baby—our sweetheart," reviews the Christmas show. It must have taken place in the empty, crumbling, closed-up theater I had just passed:

> From it's [*sic*] spirit-lifting choral beginning to it's [*sic*] shoulder shakin', moving end, the X-mas show was completely enjoyable. . . . The future for Three Notes would be assured with proper management and polish . . . their delivery of *Walking by the River* and *I Laughed at Love* were quite good, perhaps better, than vocal groups on the scene today . . . the talented R. Marrero, the young man who gives a fine dramatic recitation of Gunga Din, has empathy, a prized quality in the theatrical world . . . Mr. Parrish does very good work with *Caravan* and *All the Way* with a most interesting vibrato that could sell records.

So many happy, bright possibilities in all their futures.

There's a section called "They're Talking About," with entries like "They're talking about . . . cutting down the bread to three slices—to see who really loves pigeons."

One of the old buildings used to be a toy-repair shop where elderly and infirm inmates repaired toys to give to poor children on Christmas morning. A *Daily News* photographer took pictures for a story in the 1950s. Men in suits and a woman in a nice hat pose with the inmates as they work. They're all very proud.

The pictures are creepy. In one shot everyone is standing in front of a primitive painting of a wild man tearing his hair out. In another they hover over an old inmate struggling to sew a doll's dress back together. She's missing a foot and three fingers on one hand. Even if that prisoner did manage to fix the hole in the dress, she was still going to be an old doll with one foot and some missing fingers. Did they really think some little girl was going to be thrilled to get her? Although I could see a child loving the doll in a misfit-toy kind of way.

The next building we came to was a chapel. An article in the October 25, 1931, *New York Times* talked about a cornerstone being laid for a Catholic chapel. A thousand prisoners and eight hundred "prominent" men attended the ceremonies, according to the *Times*. The prisoners' band played and their choir sang. Someone identified as the "Right Rev. Mgr. Lavelle, vicar general of the archdiocese of New York and rector of St. Patrick's Cathedral," spoke. "This chapel for years to come will teach every one who enters it the wisdom of an unspoiled life. It will teach each man that he must live according to high ideals if he wants to find happiness in the world. We all hope and pray that this work will be a success and that of all men who enter its doors not one will return to this or any other penal institution." Oh, brother.

It was estimated that the chapel would cost $60,000 to build, but I couldn't find a later article that announced either success or failure. But there it was, right in front of me: raised, completed, used, and then abandoned, boarded up, and slowly crumbling. Over the chapel door, in great big letters, were the same letters that appeared on my grandmother Daisy's grave: IHS. It took about a dozen calls to various churches around the city before I found a priest from St. Mark's Orthodox Monastery to explain that they were the first three letters of "Jesus Christ" in Greek (and not an acronym for I Hate Stacy).

Next up was Kratter's Field, a ballpark where no one plays ball any more. It was named for Marvin Kratter, a builder who owned the site of Ebbets Field (where he built an apartment building) and who donated the original bleachers to the Hart Island ballpark. When the bleachers were installed they held a big ceremony, capped off by a game between the prisoners' team and a team from the Nike missile base. The game was tied at 5–5 when it was called because of the 3:50 P.M. prisoner count. You can still make out home plate, second base, and where the bleachers once sat—on ties taken from the dismantled Third Avenue El.

Nothing was left of the Nike missile base except the cemented-over entrance to the missile silo, which Ruppert wouldn't even let me stand on (I was trying to figure out a way to get down inside).

The baby trench was last. It's in the middle of a large green field with purple asters and other wildflowers that Melinda, Ruppert, and I didn't know the names of. The markers sit in rows under willow trees, next to a tall white monument to the Civil War dead who are no longer there, and all of it, the babies, the flowers, and the former site of the Union dead, is within a hundred yards of the sea. Later I was able to tell Sue Rosen truthfully, "She's in a beautiful spot. And she's not alone, she's with lots of other children." Sue cried when I told her. "All the babies are together on one of the nicest spots on the island," I continued. It's not that I wanted to stop her from crying. It's just that she told me that she thought sending her daughter to Hart Island was like throwing her in the trash, and I wanted her to know that she was really and truly wrong. In a cemetery she'd have been trapped and all alone in her solitary box, separate from the dead and even more separate from the living, who could never really be near her even if they visited every day. On Hart Island she is together with thousands of other babies in a field of wildflowers and green and waves so loud we had to scream to be heard, and nothing about the spot—not us, not the place—screams "dead."

The prisoners treat the dead babies, and all those buried on Hart Island, with care, respect, and even tenderness. Melinda explained that this was because they believe they will themselves eventually be buried there, along with their families, friends, and neighbors. They place flowers, crosses, and fruit at the foot of a statue of the Madonna.

I talked to Sue again a few weeks later to tell her that the records for August 1957, when her daughter was buried, had been destroyed. I had promised I would find Michelle's record and I shouldn't have. I felt just awful, but Sue Rosen no longer cares. She doesn't have this little nightmare any longer. She doesn't cry, she isn't disappointed. My visit seems to have brought her peace. Everyone moves on but me.

cats

B EAMERS OFFICIALLY has every cat affliction known. One morning he curled up on the floor next to me while I was working and couldn't get back up. I watched him paw the ground for a minute, trying to stand, clawing the ground, trying to raise his head, struggling, flailing. I hoped he was playing or something—I was desperate for him to be playing or something—but he honestly tried to get up and couldn't. My cat couldn't stand. His legs wouldn't work. He was looking at me. Of course he was scared. I wished I could talk to him. I wished I could tell him that I was taking him to the doctor and that everything would be okay. *Don't be scared, honey.* I grabbed him and ran to the vet.

They told me to have a seat. I started to, but I didn't think there was time to waste. I told them he was diabetic and that he was having some weird kind of seizure. I'd never seen him act like that and they had to look at him now. *Now.* I tried not to scream at them. "I think the doctor should look at him now," I said again.

The woman could tell I was trying not to scream, and she got the doctor, who performed an immediate blood test. It wasn't insulin shock. Beamers's levels were fine. But he couldn't stand five minutes ago, I said. If only Beamers could explain his symptoms. How many times has something you've said helped the doctor figure out what was wrong with you? I used to wonder how parents could stand it when their children were sick if it caused me this much pain when the sick one was my cat. You can at least talk to your children. You can get specifics. You can ask them if they're scared and you can explain things to them. "We think it's his thyroid," they told me, handing me a sheet of paper explaining the various treatment options if that turned out to be the case.

It did. I now had to add a quarter tablet of the thyroid medicine twice a day to the Beamers Health Regimen. Four or five years would be a spectacular run for a cat with kidney disease, Dr. Sullivan had told me. But it's probably too much to hope for in a cat with kidney disease, diabetes, a thyroid condition, and a stomach thing I still can't remember the name of.

Nostalgia

I'LL NEVER LEARN. Christmas was back and I still thought I'd find redemption through the holidays. The problem wasn't with the idea, I decided. I was going about it all wrong. It's like the movie *Groundhog Day*. In the movie Bill Murray lives the same day over and over. *If only life were like that*, I remember thinking. *If only we had the opportunity to live the same day again and again and again until we got it right*. Then it hit me: we do. The problem is we wake up thinking *Whole new day* when really, one day is pretty much the same as the last and we do in fact have the opportunity to do something, anything, differently. If it doesn't get us to where we want to be, that's okay—everything will be the same again tomorrow. As long as we continue to live, we'll always have another chance to try something else, and we can keep trying until we wake up to a day we actually do want to live, and relive.

We're so tragically oblivious, though, and change is so hard, that we rarely take advantage of this repeated opportunity. Every Christmas I was disappointed because every Christmas I did the exact same thing. I had to do something different. It didn't need to be *big* different—who knew what the effects of even the tiniest change would be? What should I try? Where did it all start to go wrong? If only I could line up the ghosts of my Christmas Past, Present, and Future, I might be able to change the shadows of what might be. I decided to do *A Christmas Carol* in Bizarro World. It was a little different.

My friend Chris and I started at the Oke Doke Restaurant, which isn't a restaurant but a bar. I used to go there when I was in my early twenties—when I first started making the mistakes I'm still making now. The Oke Doke is a tiny bar on Manhattan's Upper East Side, and Elsie, the owner, doesn't open the door for everyone. You knock, she looks you over, and then maybe she'll let you in. We got to the block. The last time I went there I was twenty-five; it was darker and smaller than I'd remembered. I almost walked right by. Chris was sure the place was closed. I knew "closed" was a relative concept for Elsie. I looked in the window, trying to assume a let-in-able expression. This seemed to have worked. Elsie buzzed us inside.

The place was practically unchanged. The same singers were on the jukebox: Frank Sinatra, who is the most heavily represented, Al Jolson, Patsy Cline, Bobby Darin, Mario Lanza, the Ink Spots, and Peggy Lee. I recognized the few knick-knacks behind the bar, like the cheap brandy snifter filled with twenty-year-old, now smell-less potpourri, as well as the shufflebowl game on the way to the bathroom. Nothing had been moved in eighteen years, nothing had been spruced up, nothing had been renovated. It was dingier and less cheerful, but the Oke Doke Restaurant had just given me my first Christmas glimpse of redemption. It was the same, I was still around, and maybe I would have the chance to alter the course of Christmases yet to be.

Elsie poured Chris a watered-down Jameson's and me a glass of flat seltzer water. She was smaller than I remembered, and grayer. The everything-is-smaller-than-you-remembered thing is not only a childhood phenomena, and it doesn't just apply to houses, schools, and trees. Unless, of course, Elsie had genuinely shrunk, which is more than possible. "I've been running this place since 1950," she told me. "I remember you," she added. I didn't care whether this was true or not. I liked that she said it. She told me that the guys I used to come in here with—who weren't exactly the nicest guys in the world— still came around. She clearly adored them. She called them "my boys" and told me what they are all up to. I loved that these guys—guys I don't particularly like—were still around and still stopped in to drink at Elsie's.

The three of us talked about men and children until she buzzed in a group of six young Eastern European men who, recognizing the honor they had been given, thanked her very politely, and took the stools to our right. A little while later she buzzed in a handsome man roughly my age who walked in with a very lovely young woman in her twenties. They sat to my left. "This is my third time in there this week," he announced to the room. I liked him at once. I started to talk to him, but he seemed uncomfortable, so I turned back to Chris. Again, he addressed the room. "I've been coming here for a long time." Elsie pulled out a guest book in response. "Someone gave this to me in 1986," she said, handing it to the couple. It lists dates, names, and addresses, and, best part, has a space for comments. The young woman started turning the pages. I leaned over. I knew she was just being nice—she didn't care about the book—and I was impatient for her to give it to me. *Hurry up, lovely person.* Finally she did.

I scanned for familiar names. Then I started reading the

comments aloud. I found one of Elsie's boys, someone I used to come here with, and she asked me what he'd written. "You haven't read these comments?" I asked her. She hadn't. "I will always love you . . . Your Tallboy." (He was gigantic, I remember.) I found his brother's name. He'd written, "When will I be known only for my own good deeds?" A touching question. I read the comments of parents who signed her book and thanked her for taking care of their children.

Chris was ready to leave. I wanted to stay and read every last comment. I wanted to try to talk to the man to my left again. But we'd been there a couple of hours and this was my *Christmas Carol* in Bizarro World, not Chris's. She'd been very patient. I started putting on my coat. Chris told me later that the man to my left looked pained as we were leaving and that he'd tried to catch my eye but I was looking at Elsie. When I'd first walked in, I'd immediately started taking notes. "You better not be writing about me," Elsie warned me. I put my notes away. As we were leaving, Elsie said, "You can write about me." A tiny moment of glory. I can come back. I wish I had turned to the man and said, "Look for me," but tomorrow will be exactly the same and maybe I will say it then.

Next up was the Shore Hotel on Coney Island, where the spirits of my Christmas Future seem to huddle among buildings that have seen better days. I dream of living out my twilight years here. Someday I'd like to buy and renovate one of the many decaying buildings in the once-glittering amusement park and turn it into a retirement home for me and all my friends. We'll walk along the mostly abandoned boardwalk and beach and attractions and live where no one else wants to live, so it shouldn't cost too much.

The Shore Hotel is located on Surf Avenue, directly in front of the amusement rides, which were chained up for the winter and silent. The entrance is on an alley called Henderson's Walk, named for Fred Henderson, who once owned a restaurant and music hall here. It sits opposite the former Surf Hotel, which opened for business in 1929. (When I was flipping through the *New York Times* index to look up these places, after looking up "Shore" and on my way to "Surf" I came across the "suicide" entry. Column after column of suicides, going back a century. For comparison, I looked up "suicide" in the *Times of London* index. Two listings. We're either far more self-destructive or far, far more interested in the subject.) The Shore Hotel, which rents by the hour, has been in business since 1984.

I got there at dusk and was a little afraid. I wasn't even sure I wanted to walk the twenty feet down the alley to the door of the hotel. No one was around. I heard a high-pitched hum that was either something electrical or the wind moving through something empty. But it was so cold, and I'd come all this way. I chanced it. The rates were posted outside: thirty-two dollars for a short stay, fifty-two dollars if you wanted to stay all night. Someone buzzed me in. I climbed the stairs and then immediately chickened out. There was something off about the eyes of the guy who asked, "Can I help you?" I wanted to know what the deal was with his eyes, but it would have been rude to look to closely so I didn't. "I'd like a room for a short stay, please." I couldn't spend the night. There seemed to be not a hint of warmth or humanity to the Shore Hotel—it was a hotel in Purgatory, a place where the as-good-as-dead stay. That was my first impression. Then, through my nervousness, I could see the guy with something wrong with his eyes was kind of nice and a little shy.

He let me into a room on that floor, two doors down from the office. But I couldn't get the lights to work. I had to go back and get him, and he showed me how to flip this switch, not that one, and jiggle it. There were no blankets on the bed, only one sheet, two pillows, and a stack of towels. The blankets were on the dresser, along with a woman's scrunchy and a bobby pin. The mirror above the sink was covered with Spice Girls stickers and in the sink were two used soaps. There was a refrigerator in the room but it wasn't turned on and when I opened it, it smelled bad. The radiator, which was meant to sit on the floor, was bolted to the wall about a foot and a half off the ground. The heat coming up sounded like bells.

You could hear the subway constantly, which was weird because whenever I've been on Coney Island, it felt like forever between trains. Footsteps walked by my door about once or twice a minute. *Now what?* This was a very poorly planned trip. I went over to the window. The view was of the boarded-up Surf Hotel. Maybe that's the building I should fix up for me and my twilight-years friends. It looked as if it'd been empty for decades, but I found out later it had only been six years. I turned and looked at my room. It was a sad little room, but the initial panic had worn off and I'd switched to thinking that I could make myself comfortable here. I could make it home. Clean it, paint it, buy new sheets and blankets, put in a TV and something to play music, get each of my friends to take the other rooms so we can drink coffee and gossip and watch our favorite shows together. You can make yourself happy anywhere.

But I was restless. I wanted to look around. I went out into the hall to find someone to talk to. "Can I . . . help you?" a woman asked me tentatively. She was on her way to do laundry. I was nervous again. "I'm looking for the guy who gave me my room." She called out and a different person, a big guy, appeared, but he seemed nice, too, so I talked to him. His name was Dimos. He was the owner and lived there with his wife and two teenage children. He took me around the different floors and even up to the roof, where I had the best view of the park and all the motionless rides. On the Astro Tower was a great big white glowing Star of David. On the Wonder Wheel was a fuchsia cross. *Maybe. Maybe.* I always loved the crumbling decay of New Orleans, but Coney Island seemed seedier. And flimsier. The people here seemed more desperate than decadent. Still, Coney Island has its own kind of beauty. It's a Charlie Brown Christmas tree of a place. It just needs some affection. I pictured my friends and me up here on the roof, sitting on lawn chairs, sipping cocktails.

I wanted to walk around the park, but Dimos didn't think I should go alone and offered to go with me. "I couldn't impose." "I wasn't doing anything else." It was even colder than before. The wind was coming up over the Atlantic—why hadn't I remembered to bring a hat? Everything was boarded up. I thought something might stay open through the winter—the Coney Island Circus Sideshow, for instance, which is held in a small indoor theater. But no. We headed back and I saw the words "Paradise by the Sea" stenciled in black letters along the gutter of the Shore Hotel. "Did you put that there?" I asked him. He did. He calls the Shore Hotel paradise. Inside, he introduced me to his wife and children and I thought, *I could feel safe here.*

But I wanted to get into the old Surf Hotel. What if the Shore Hotel didn't pan out? I needed to scout out other locations for my future rest home. I'd tracked down the current owner of the building and both written him and left messages but I hadn't heard anything. I went back a few days later to see if I could find a way inside without him.

Another freezing cold day. I walked around the Surf Hotel twice. Some of the red and blue lightbulbs that surround the fading sign over the front door were still intact. Everything was battened down, though. I couldn't find a way in. Then, a few streets down, I found it—the future Stacy Horn & Friends Retirement Home: a long, narrow building sitting in an abandoned field on Surf Avenue, between Fifteenth and Kensington, where the timber of the old Thunderbolt Roller Coaster from 1926 slowly falls apart and the Parachute Jump sits and rusts. You can still make out the sign over the door—"Playland." Plastic lawn chairs were already sitting outside for me and all my friends to wash off and while away the day. A dog barked as I walked around, trying to find a break in the fence. Weeds and red berries came up through the cracking asphalt. Electrical wires hung everywhere, unconnected. The whole place had that dark, romantic *Carnival of Souls* feel of desolation, and I couldn't wait for the Christmas Future when we could all move in.

Now all I had left were the spirits of Christmas Present. I was down to the wire. On Christmas Eve, I went over to the nursing home to visit Lotte, my former neighbor. She was having a terrible holiday. I had only started visiting her a few months ago and already she'd gone from looking eightyish to looking one hundred–ish. At one point she said, "They won't just let you die." I decided my Christmas present would be to listen to whatever she wanted to say. "You would like to die, Lotte?" She told me what life was like for her now, and there didn't seem to be much to look forward to. I didn't want to lie and make up stuff to be cheerful about. Besides, I was trying to fight an anxiety attack. At one point she said, "They won't get me what I want!" And I thought, *Oh good, I can go get something for her.* "What? What do you want?" I asked. "Freedom," she answered.

The guy sitting across from us was missing half his skull. It was as if someone had taken a large ice cream scoop to his head. I don't know how you can live with half a skull like that. He held his fist up in the air almost the entire time I was there. He was growling but I think he may have been trying to talk or scream. "He's mean," Lotte told me. "I would be, too," I said. But Lotte was not feeling in much better shape, even if her skull was intact. A half-dozen people sat staring at the walls. Only one person seemed actually to be watching the TV set that was on. Anyone giving any sign of being alert was watching me and Lotte.

The nursing home stank of urine. I can still smell it. Normally it didn't smell as strong as that. But it was Christmas Eve, and I think this is how the people there handle the holidays. The rest of us get low-grade flu symptoms, or become short-tempered and frazzled. People in these places lose control. Who's going to listen to their complaints? The only thing left to them is letting go.

Then this big, booming nurse who sounded Jamaican came in and hugged and kissed the man with half a head. She was all over him, saying his name over and over. I could barely look at him, and she was kissing him. He stopped growling and smiled. He looked happy. I'd been thinking that he was dead, that all that was left of him was anger, but clearly someone was still alive in there. He could tell the difference between a good thing—being hugged and kissed by this wonderful nurse—and a bad thing—being left to stare at a wall and try to scream. Were the ghosts of my Christmas Present foreshadowing my Christmas Future? Was this nursing home my future, and not the Stacy Horn & Friends Retirement Home on Coney Island?

I felt just like Scrooge in that scene where the silent Spirit of Christmas Future shows him his grave. Scrooge cowers over the newly turned earth. "Before I draw nearer to that stone," he begs, "answer me one question. Are these the shadows of things that must be? Or are they only the shadows of things that might be? I know that men's deeds foreshadow certain ends, but if the deeds be departed from, surely the ends will change. Tell it is so with what you show me now." Meaning the tombstone. Why does Dickens toy with us like that? Do we have to die? Yes. If we're really really good can we live forever? No. There's no way out. Scrooge can change the quality of what remains of his life but there's nothing he can do about that tombstone. This scene disturbed me as a child and it disturbs me now. I can take steps to improve my chances of getting to the Stacy Horn & Friends Retirement Home someday, but will I get from there to here with half a skull?

I wonder if all my best Christmases are truly in my future. What about now? This year, instead of staying home alone on Christmas Eve I went out with friends, but I only felt a little different. I told myself it took Bill Murray a lot of time and plenty of tries in *Groundhog Day* to get results he could live with, and managed to feel hopeful. *I'm going to figure this out.* I poured a fresh cup of cold water for my ghost, turned off the lamps and turned on the Christmas lights, then watched *Mr. Magoo's Christmas Carol* with my fed, injected, and all-taken-care-of Veets and Beams. "Merry Christmas, Veets. Merry Christmas, Beams."

cats

Six days later Veets died. I wish I had remembered to tell him, "I'll be back," before he died. It was another ritual of ours, one I got from a book called *The Natural Cat*. Whenever I left the house I'd look at Veets and Beams and say, "I'll be back." Then I'd do the eye-blinking thing that we all liked and list the things we'd do when I returned: food, hugs, kisses, and curling up on the couch to watch TV, birds, and airplanes. Beams never cared about the "I'll be back" ritual, but Veets would always look up and half close his eyes, as if already dreaming of the good times ahead. "I'll be back" was for him. "I may be going away," I was telling him, "but I will always come back for you." Instead, during his very last minute alive I kept saying, "I love you" and "Thank you," which isn't bad, but I like "I'll be back" better and I think he would have been more comforted by that.

The Monday after Christmas I took Veets to the Cat Practice and what we thought might have been the flu turned out to be cancer that was everywhere. Dr. Sullivan showed me the X-rays and later, the sonogram, and told me Veets had anywhere from a couple of days to a couple of months left to live.

ME: How can that be? He was absolutely fine a couple of days ago.
VET: Cats are good hiders.
ME: But he looks fine. He looks better than he's ever looked.

I wanted to say, "No, no, no, no, no," and "Fuck you." Not to Dr. Sullivan. Sometimes I wish I believed in God—not just for the great things, such as life after death, but because it would feel so satisfying to have someone really, officially in charge to blame. "No, no, no, no, no." I looked on the Internet, I read books, I made phone calls, they took more tests. What I found gave me every reason to hope. I made an appointment to see a feline oncologist, then got the apartment ready for my sick Veets and a miracle. I put a box with a blanket by the radiator. I bought extra treats and catnip. I cleared space on a shelf for all his medications and taped the instructions for his care next to exhaustive directions for both Veets and Beams labeled: "In Case I Die." (I panicked one day, thinking *What if I die and someone takes my cats without knowing they have to do all this stuff?*) I got a subcutaneous drip spot ready next to where Beams gets his drip and looked forward to giving Veets as much medical attention as I have always given Beams. I would nurse him back to health and we'd grow even more unnaturally close by the happy end of it all.

But I was also realistic. I saw how much the cancer had progressed—and there was the diabetes, his age. I called around until I found a veterinarian who would come to my house to put him to sleep (my veterinarian was not insured to do this). My worst-case scenario gave us a few more months together. When I took him home he looked so good I asked my friend Jackie if she would come over and take a video of me and him and Beams before his illness started to show.

I put him to sleep the next day—New Year's Eve, 1999. On the morning of January 1, 2000, my friend Joe said, "Veets was not Y2K compliant."

Of course it was nothing like I imagined it would be. There was no ice cream and fish. He wasn't eating anymore. There were no Ping-Pong ball games. He wasn't moving. I woke up on New Year's Eve ready to begin the road to recovery and instead found Veets in his basket by the radiator, struggling to breathe. I made phone calls, looked on the Internet, read some more in my books. There was no reason to hope. I called the vet, the one who said she could come to my home, and told her this was it. Veets jumped up onto the chair that I sit in every day and never moved to another spot again. We sat and waited all day for her to arrive. Hour after hour. Veets kept getting worse. It was so fast. I read to him. I knew it didn't matter what I read so I pulled out Shirley Jackson's *We Have Always Lived in the Castle*, because it was closest. I sang to him. I talked to him. Then I left him alone because I thought that was what he really wanted. I could tell he wasn't listening to me anymore. My poor little cat. I couldn't reach him. The night before, he'd jumped up on the couch and curled into my stomach, just like he always used to, only he didn't stay there very long. After about twenty minutes he went back to his spot by the radiator. I think that was my good-bye.

His steady, rhythmic gasping continued. I went from *I want my cat to live forever* to *For God's sake take the poor thing now*. At around noon I went out and got him medication so he could rest easier. It seemed to help but what little movement he was making was over. I watched TV very, very quietly and waited.

At one point the song "Beyond the Blue Horizon" came on the television. I thought the world couldn't possibly be more terrible.

Beamers stayed in the bedroom the whole time.

When the vet arrived, she gave him his first shot right away, to calm him. "He looks so robust," she said when she saw him. What? "Maybe it's too soon," I cried, feeling the sickening, unanswerable horror of doubt, which has never gone away. I want him to have all the time he has coming to him. Should I have done this tomorrow? Next week? "No, no," she assured me. "He's never going to get better, only worse." Then we cleared my desk so she could have a flat surface and light to work with. Now it's the place where my baby Veets died. She put a line into his leg. He cried. *Oh God*, I thought. *You're scaring him. You're hurting him.* "He's not tranquilized enough," I told her. She gave him some more. "Look how much I'm giving him," she said, trying to make me feel better. We were huddled together in such an awful, deadly intimacy. I started the "I love yous" and "Thank yous," but Veets wasn't moving, he wasn't hearing. I petted him. I couldn't make him purr. We were both so happy yesterday when I came to take him home. The day before he purred and purred.

Beyond the blue horizon waits a beautiful day.

The vet had an easy time finding a vein. I thought, *No one has to don gloves to give shots to my little green-dot kitty ever again.* Then she injected him with whatever it was that killed him. I looked over and watched a small pink cloud erupt into the IV like a tiny atom bomb and I knew I only had a few seconds left. *Fourteen years are wrapping up. This is it. The unthinkable is happening right now.* I kissed his tiny body, petted him, looked at his shaved, exposed, gray, flabby, vulnerable belly, desperate to protect him and desperate to stop trying so I could make one last connection and somehow sum up all my love and gratitude in these last few seconds, to find the one word or gesture

246

that might possibly make dying okay. *Good-bye, good-bye, good-bye, I love you forever and thank you, Petey.* (Another one of my names for him.) He made a loud sigh. I wasn't looking into his face, I was watching his chest. I couldn't kiss him again, because I knew. It was that fast. There. Not there. The light of my life. Out. The vet touched his eyeball to be sure; then she tried to close his eyes but they wouldn't stay closed. She kept trying. She was doing this for me. "Please stop," I said. I started kissing him again. I half stood and then sat back down again. I looked into his dead eyes and said, "Come back?" But he was never coming back from what I'd just done to him. *I'm so sorry, my baby Veets.* I don't know what time he died. I didn't look. Sometime between 4:40 and 5:00. I had the rest of New Year's Eve ahead of me, hours in which to contemplate ringing in the new year, the new millennium, the rest of my life, without my beloved little Veets.

The guy from the crematory came within minutes. He and the vet exchanged familiar, old-friends smiles in the hall. I didn't want him picking up Veets, so I lifted him myself. Mistake. I'd never held a dead thing before. He felt like a warm, oversized Beanie Baby, weighted with liquid and stone. There was a stain on my desk where his leg had been, maybe from the alcohol the vet rubbed on his skin before inserting the IV. The crematory guy said, "Wrap him up in his favorite thing." I looked around for a favorite thing and saw his favorite blanket, but instead I gave the guy a sweater Veets'd liked to sleep on. Then I hated myself because the only reason I gave him the sweater was because I didn't want to sacrifice the whole entire blanket. I'm glad I still have the blanket, because it's something Veets loved, but it will always be a reminder that I wouldn't give up a blanket for him. *Hate. Hate. Hate. Self.*

When the crematory guy left, Beams came out for the first time and sniffed the spot on the floor where Veets had been lying in the bag he was carried away in.

I started spinning around, looking for Veets, like I might actually find him. Like he hadn't just been carried out in a shoulder bag. Gone, completely gone, is a hard thing to understand at first. Absence is hard to see. I saw towels, blankets, impressions in pillows, cat hair. Something was hovering over and above me and it was going to flatten me. I kept spinning. There must be something here to protect me. Where? What? I didn't want to feel it. Towels, blankets, pillows, WHAT? *There.* In front of the sink and next to the tins of cat food that Veets would never eat: a gray, plastic food bowl, as tender as a black, diabetic cat. Undeniable proof that I would never feed him again. He was not going to come running up when I so much as glanced in the direction of the kitchen. Food! Food! Food! No more food for Petey. I ran out the door and walked until walking started to make me feel worse—*I've got nowhere to go and no Veets to go home to*—then I went to Echo's office. I thought spending time in this place I had built would help. I used to go there when it was still empty, before we moved all our furniture and modems in, and it made me feel everything was going to be okay, the future was full of promise. But Veets was gone from there, too.

I kept thinking, *I had all my ducks in a row for what, five minutes?* My apartment had just been painted. Everything was fixed up and just the way I wanted it. I'd put up new pictures on the walls, mostly of Veets and Beams. The windows had been cleaned and hung with new, moss-green curtains. The floors had been scoured. All my books and papers and tapes and CDs were in order. On Christmas Eve I had sat on the couch and thought, *My life isn't perfect but it's basically okay because I have a nice, clean, freshly painted apartment, a TV, this pumpkin pie I special-ordered from my favorite bakery, and, most of all, Veets and Beams.* When Veets hadn't finished his dinner Christmas night I called the vet. "It's probably an upper respiratory thing that is going around," he had said. "Bring him in on Monday, it's not serious." *Everything is going to be okay.* So I ate my pie, happy that everything seemed almost just about right. It hadn't lasted a week.

Over the next few days Chris kept calling, knowing that I might not be able to talk. Mauro sent me a poem. The Cat Practice sent a condolence card. My friend Marianne, who has a Web site for children, dedicated an animal story to Veets. Anthony Scotti from the Bay Shore Funeral Home called. "You should have told me. I would have taken care of him for you." "You do pets?" I asked. "No. But I would have made an exception for Veets." In the Secret Space, Mikal wrote, "Your ghost felt awful about Veets." My ghost, who supposedly did not like cats? "The ghost has had a change of heart about cats," Mikal explained. Jim said, "The ghost takes care of Veets now."

Two weeks later Veets was returned in a white cardboard carton with a pink silk rose pinned to the top. The label reads, "Beloved Veets." *Cat. Box. Cat. Box.* It was like a song I couldn't get out of my head. The container that actually holds his ashes is made of tin, with pink flowers and green leaves on the cover. There's a certificate inside that says he was cremated according to the rules and regulations of the State of New York, on January 4, 1999. (They got the year wrong.) *Cat. Box. Cat. Box. I've got a box. Instead of a cat.* His ashes are beige and they come to maybe a quarter or a third of a cup. I keep them on the shelf next to the place where I always hid his food between meals. I like that he is sitting on the shelf he always wanted to reach.

I called my friend Chris. "I want my cat back," I said.

"Everyone wants something back," she replied.

MUSIC

"**B**EYOND THE BLUE HORIZON" Words by Leo Robin, music by Richard A. Whiting and W. Franke Harling.

Blow, whistle blow away,
Blow away the past.
Go engine anywhere.
I don't care how fast.
On, on from darkness into dawn,
From rain into the rainbow,
Fly with me.
Gone, gone all my grief and woe.
What matter where I go if I am free?

Beyond the blue horizon
Waits a beautiful day.

Goodbye to things that bore me.
Joy is waiting for me.
I see a new horizon.
My life has only begun.
Beyond the blue horizon lies a rising sun.

deatH

I FORGOT THAT SORROW isn't strictly an emotion, that it also involves real, physical pain. Low-level pain. It's worse than a cold, but not as bad as pneumonia. Although I am perfectly capable of spending two weeks immobile on the couch for no good reason—okay, it's one of my favorite things—I spent the two weeks after Veets's death lying there with Beamers, not simply because my heart ached but because so did everything else. I couldn't do much of anything. I asked my friends to look after Echo and I only left the couch for food and supplies.

It gave me plenty of time to think. Before Veets died, I had believed that I had made some real progress with the end of the first half of my life, that what happiness I had found was genuine and internal. But now I saw that it had all depended on a couple of cats. One was dead, and the other would soon follow. I was sure I would never be happy again. I logged into the Secret Space and took a poll.

ME: Am I a freak?
JOE: Yes.
MARIANNE: No.
HOWARD: No.
MIKAL: No.
EVERYONE ELSE BUT JOE: No.

I obsessed about every way in which I felt I had failed Veets. (A) I put him to sleep too fast. What if he had rallied? I should have driven him to the hospital and made one last valiant shot at recovery. What if a mistake had been made and he didn't really have cancer after all but a really bad case of something that he might have gotten over? Results from the last test hadn't come back yet. What if it was all one big mistake? (B) I hadn't treated him as well as Beamers. Except for the last year, he always came second to Beamers and he was such a good sport about it, too. I had cheated him. I hadn't loved him enough. Veets had been perfect. I sucked. (C) I should have never put him on that stupid diet. For a year I had had him on a strict diet because everything I read informed me that over-weight cats died younger and in very nasty ways. His longing for more food after that had been so great it had hurt to watch, but the idea that I would have had him around longer gave me strength. Total waste. I could have fed him anything he wanted.

Everything became a series of firsts. The first time I gave Beams his drip without Veets. I cried and cried and Beamers struggled because there was no Veets to lick his head to calm him down. The first time I had to buy things for just one cat, feed one cat, clean up after one cat. I still have Veets's last insulin bottle and all his unused food. I took an empty cat food tin from the garbage that held the last food I ever fed him and felt like I had rescued something of the essence of Veets. I felt love for that cat food tin. It was as if I hadn't completely lost him, because see? I have his last tin here. I'm sure there's a DSM label for what I was doing. (DSM: *The Diagnostic and Statistical Manual of Mental Disorders*, put out by the American Psychiatric Association.) I'm guessing it has to do with the word "fetish," which I've never properly understood. When the woman who cleans my house unknowingly threw it away a few weeks later it was as if I had lost my last remaining link to his still-beating heart.

For a while every smile, every laugh, felt like a betrayal. I couldn't listen to happy songs. I couldn't enjoy something funny on the TV. I still can't eat pumpkin pie. I can't eat pumpkin pie until Veets has gotten every minute, hour, day, month, and year of mourning that he deserves.

While I sat on my couch not doing much of anything, I also thought about all the things I had said I would do once I wasn't tied to giving Veets and Beams insulin injections every twelve hours. I realized, yet again, that my life wasn't about to begin, it was half over. It was just like Sue Rosen had said: "You wake up one morning and you realize, *This is it. I'm not going anywhere. I'm where I'm going to be.* That is when you really grow up." My life was what it was and I'd just lost a big part of it. I couldn't move. I was defeated. I felt like the most pathetic loser ever because my happiness had been dependent on cats. My friends were just being nice. I was a freak.

Then all these studies about pet owners started appearing. I read in the *Daily News* that, according to an American Animal Hospital Association (AAHA) survey, 53 percent of pet owners will take off work to look after a sick pet. Sixty-six percent take their pets to veterinarians more than they see doctors for themselves. A CNN report said that there are 235 million pets in the United States and that 53 percent of those pets' owners greet their pets before their spouses when they come home (the AAHA survey said 72 percent). I pulled out my calculator. One hundred twenty-four thousand five hundred and fifty million losers just like me.

Some friends said, "Get another cat." Other friends said, "Don't get another cat." At the Cat Practice, Dr. Shimel, whose specialty is feline behavior, said, "Definitely get another cat. It's the best thing for you and the best thing for Beamers." At first I thought that it was the ultimate betrayal. *Well, Veets is dead. Next?* Then I hated myself for deep-down liking the idea. I could feel a genuine reduction in the pain. I decided I had two choices. I could come clean and admit I loved my TV-cemetery-drumming-feline life, and embrace my inner loser, or I could pretend it wasn't true, and that I didn't really *need* cats, and then be miserable on top of being pathetic.

I got off my couch and started to look for a new cat.

poLL

THERE'S AN ALLY MCBEAL EPISODE in which Tracy Ullman, who plays a shrink, tells Ally to find a theme song. She tells her to find a song to play in her head, one that makes her feel better. I need to feel better, so I'm looking for my own theme song. I briefly considered "Beyond the Blue Horizon," surprisingly. It went from being the song from hell to being a song of hope. If nothing lasts and everything changes, sorrow, too, must also end. But it's Veets's death song, so I needed to find a different one.

I was thinking of going with the "Domine fili unigenite" chorus from Vivaldi's *Gloria*. The melody is perfect and it hits just the right walking-down-the-street beat, but the words are a problem. Apparently "Domine fili unigenite" translates to "Only begotten Lord and Son of God," which kinda kills it. In any case, what I find amazing is that the right piece of music can genuinely work. Not at first. Not while you're in the throes of there-should-be-no-more-beautiful-days ever. But eventually denial and wishful thinking kick in, and that's when a catchy tune can lead you out of death. Pretty fucked up, when you think about it.

From a poll of 140 people on Echo:

When things are going wrong in your life, what makes every-thing okay? Or, what at least makes you feel better? What are the things that make life worth living, or bearable, when everything else mostly sucks?
Only three people said "TV," which would have been first on my list. And only two people said the movies. One person said, "I have fun feeling sorry for myself." Fuckin' A.

Fifteen percent said music.
Thirteen percent said food.
Ten percent said their pets.
Ten percent said friends.
Nine percent said children.
Nine percent said their spouse or boyfriend or girlfriend.

cats

I ENDED UP ADOPTING the first kitten I laid eyes on. He was one of two remaining cats rescued from an abandoned beauty parlor in Harlem, where a woman lived with five cats, six kittens, and more cockroaches than the rescuer, Sally Spooner, had ever seen before. The two kittens were sitting together in a cage at the Cat Practice and while I liked them both I was more drawn to the little gray one. He blinked at me. But he wouldn't let me hold him and I was aching to hold a little kitten again. *I should see more cats. I had to make the right choice for Beams.* Dr. Shimel had told me to get another male and added, because Beams was used to being the pampered one, "Make sure you don't get another alpha cat." I thought the smaller the better, that way there'd be no confusion about who was boss, but this one wasn't all that tiny, really. I decided to keep looking, feeling guilty that although he couldn't know what was going on, I had gotten his hopes up and then rejected him.

The day they delivered Veets's ashes, my friend Marianne and I went to the Center for Animal Care and Control to look at more cats. Veets and Beams came from there and I thought I might have better luck. They didn't have any sufficiently small male kittens. I picked up two smallish cats, but neither of them felt like *the one*. I told myself to wait until I had found the kitten that felt like *the one*. But I couldn't wait. I went back to the Cat Practice. "He's a pistol," Dr. Shimel warned me about the little gray. Perfect! I put the box with Veets in my purse and the gray kitten in a borrowed carrier and took them both home. Then I didn't see the kitten again for two days. After two days of his continuous crying I began to think that maybe he was genuinely happier in that cage at the Cat Practice. For the love of God, I'm still grieving. I'm not up for this. I called him "Buddy" on a temporary basis, because I couldn't think of a real name right away. Plus I was having terrible thoughts: *Maybe I shouldn't be too hasty about giving this cat a name. A name was so . . . permanent.*

I left out food and water, but the kitten wouldn't touch it. *Great. Another cat is going to die in my care.* I tried different foods. When Veets and Beams were sick and had trouble eating, they would always eat baby food or Tender Vittles. I gave the kitten baby food and Tender Vittles. Not a bite. Two days and nights went by without evidence of his eating or drinking anything. I called the Cat Practice. "He'll come out in his own time." I tried not to cry. Veets and Beams had loved me right off. They had curled up in my arms the very first thing. *Who is this little cat? Where did he come from and why is he here?* That night I dreamed that the kitten was sleeping in a ball in Veets's favorite spot next to my stomach. I woke up in pain. The longing was unendurable. *He will never be as affectionate as Veets and we'll never*

259

be that close. The forbidden thought came. *I got the wrong cat. I should take him back.* Yet I knew I would never be able to live with myself if I did. I've got a cat that will never love me and I'm stuck with him. Then I really did cry. My crying made the kitten cry. Beamers went into the other room and hid.

The next night was the first *Sopranos* episode of the new season. I had been really looking forward to watching it. Just as it began the kitten started his sad, sad crying from underneath the couch. "What, baby? What do you want? Are you scared?" He just kept crying and crying. *Ignore him*, I thought. *I can't even remember what he looks like anymore. Just watch the TV. Nothing you say or do will matter anyway.* "Meow, meow, meow," he cried, which I heard as "Somebody help me, please?" Watching TV was out of the question. *Okay, what? WHAT?* I tried meowing back. I did my best to sound like a sad and scared cat—it's a higher-pitched meow, and it goes up at the end like a question mark. This made him cry even more, and then there was a furious burst of clawing and scratching as he squeezed himself out from beneath the couch. He watched me for a little while from a distance, still crying, but looking at me while he did, as if convinced that there was something I could do about his woes. Then he started exploring. And ate all his food. And used the litter box. Oh, good. I had been wondering whether I was going to have to train him to use the litter box.

Two days later Buddy became the most affectionate cat I have ever known. If there's an opportunity—meaning if I'm not moving—he curls up with me and purrs like a miniature machine gun. Except when he's running around tearing up the place. Anything that can be knocked over is. Anything that can be batted around is: books, staple removers, eyedroppers. When I'm writing he has to lay his head against my neck, which he can only do if I hold him up there. I've had to learn to type with one hand. Beamers hisses if Buddy tries to come near him, but I think everything's going to be okay. Buddy doesn't push it, and even though he hisses at him during the day, Beamers will let Buddy sleep with his head against Beamers's stomach at night. *Where did you come from, you amazing little cat?* I called the Cat Practice. They told me they got him from a rescue outfit called City Critters. City Critters, in turn, directed me to Sally Spooner, the woman who had actually rounded up Buddy and all the the other cats. I called her. "Go up to Seventh Avenue, between 123rd and 124th Streets, and look for a beauty parlor sign with a picture of an Afro-American woman," she instructed me. I found it, across from projects called the Ennis Francis Houses and between a Laundromat and another abandoned building. The woman in the sign looked like she could also be Latina. The sign read, "Miss Ruth Presents... A Touch From Angie's Hands. Hair & Nails. 123rd Barber Shop." The windows were cemented over. A brown gate completely blocked the front of the store and a blue phone booth with a broken phone sat to the right. I looked inside but I could only see my reflection in the glass behind the gate. A guy walked by. "Hey, bitch, get off my stick." "Now, come on," another guy said. "You don't know her." I never go to Harlem, but I loved what I saw. I want to live here. (Note to self: Harlem. Another possible location for the Stacy Horn & Friends Retirement Home?)

Now, every night, while I sit immobile on the couch, Buddy moves from spot to spot as fast as he possibly can, always knocking something over, and then batting around whatever falls.

Crash. A religious triptych that sits on my coffee table.
Pause.
Bat for a minute.
Run.
Crash. A container of pens and pencils on my desk.
Pause.
Bat like crazy. A batting frenzy.

Run.

Crash. The telephone.

Pause.

Bat for a second. Not bat-able.

Run.

Crash. My glasses.

Pause.

Bat for a minute.

Run.

The name Buddy stuck. That's okay. Buddy's a good name. His list of names will grow. I've just added "Buddy's Sirloin Pit" after that restaurant in Cambridge I used to love. I sniff his head to see how his smell compares to Beamers's. Buddy smells like grape soda. (Beamers, you will remember, smells like leaves.) Mikal says, "The ghost loves Buddy." I remind him once more that this is the ghost that doesn't like cats. "I kept telling you," he answers, "that the ghost wanted a baby in the house. Now it has one."

work

"EVERYONE THINKS they're going to be someone special," Sue Rosen says, and I believe she's right. But when I look at all these people doing things that don't look like so much fun, and remember all the people I've heard say, "I hate my job," I can't help wondering why so few even try to find something they might enjoy more. Okay, most aren't going to make it. I probably will never work in television. But what stops them from trying?

I got my treatments for two TV shows to where Betsy and I both liked them and we sent them to the first agents Betsy didn't hate. They told Betsy that they were very excited about my shows. I was supposed to meet them that very Saturday, when they were in New York. They never called. When they were back in Los Angeles they told Betsy, "Oh, we tried to reach her and then it was Friday, and oh, we'll call her right away." They also told her they didn't care much for my shows, but liked what they'd read of *Waiting for My Cats to Die* and maybe we could make a show out of that. The agents and I played telephone tag for a couple of weeks. When one of them finally reached me she spoke exactly as I had always imagined a Hollywood agent would.

AGENT: Oh, we *love* you. You are a *great* writer. You are amazing. We love everything. We really want to work with you!
ME: What are you talking about? What do you love?

Betsy'd said they only liked my book, so I was confused.

AGENT: *Sycamore Hill.*
ME: I didn't write *Sycamore Hill.*

I hear an immediate, furious rustling of pages. I wait a bit but she's stopped talking.

ME: You don't know who you're talking to, do you?

More furious rustling of pages.

AGENT : Staaaaccccccy Horrrnnn.

She's drawing it out as long as she can while she searches and searches for something with my name on it, I'm guessing. I could see myself doing the same thing. Not the "We *love* you" part but the mixing-up-who-I'm-talking-to part. I tried to help. I gave her the titles of everything Betsy had sent her but she was completely flustered by this point, and even though I was laughing and doing everything I could to show her I didn't care that she didn't know who she was talking to, she was determined to bluff it out. "Yes, we really *love* your stuff and we'd

like to show it around and see what kind of feedback we get."
"Okay," I replied. We started talking about one of my shows.
It was like talking to a psychic. I was feeding her the facts.

ME: So you liked the one about cyberspace?
AGENT: Yes, that's the one we loved.
ME: I can't believe there isn't an Internet show on the
air already.
AGENT: Oh, us too, an Internet show. Where are all the
Internet shows?
ME: I was thinking of changing the age of the main char-
acter from middle-aged to twentysomething. I think peo-
ple in their twenties are the real market for an Internet
show.
AGENT: Yes. Twenties. Better.

Betsy talked to her later, after she'd collected her thoughts
and my writing, and she told Betsy that now they liked the
treatment for the Internet show—*Virtually Yours*—and they still
liked *Waiting for My Cats to Die*.

"I told them okay," Betsy says. "But I'm going to send your
stuff elsewhere in the meantime. Does that sound like a good
plan?" I tell her it sounds like a very good plan. She sends
everything around but everyone likes *Waiting for My Cats to Die*
best, so we decide to wait.

romance

TIM, MY EDITOR, thinks I should get in touch with Ruben Blades. My first thought is, *How humiliating.* It's not like I haven't already fantasized that he will read my book and we'll fall in love and I'll wear that Vera Wang wedding gown, but I'm pretty sure he's married. Track him down? Wouldn't that finally and firmly move me into stalker territory? "Okay," I say.

I called my friend Aly, the one who introduced me to Blades twenty years ago when he interviewed him for Reuters. "How do you pronounce his name anyway?" I figure this was an important point to clear up if I was going to try to talk to him. I'd always pronounced it "Blah-des" but everyone else says "Blades," like knife blades. Aly said it was pronounced "Blah-des" in South America but that here they said (knife) "Blades" and that's how he'd heard Ruben Blades pronounce it. So (knife) Blades it is.

"Is he married?" I asked Aly. "I don't think so," he replied, then he told me what a sweet, sweet man Blades was. "Call his record label. Find out the name of his publicist." The number for Sony rang forever, so I called the Screen Actors Guild and got the number of his agent. I left a message. When I got through to a machine for the person at Sony who might know Blades's publicist I left a message for her, too. Then I waited. No response.

The next time I called his agent I was transferred to someone named Lisa but got her assistant, who said, "Go ahead and fax what you've got." (My editor suggested sending the chapter where I describe my fantasy about him.)

I faxed everything, then immediately logged into the Secret Space to show them what I'd sent. Then I took a poll.

ME: What do you think?
JOE: (Gag.)
HOWARD: Shut up, Joe. You're a brave writer, Stacy.
ME: Oh, God. That means it's insane and he'll think so, too.
HOWARD: No, he'll be charmed and complimented and will want very badly to know what you look like.
MARIANNE: I agree with Howard.
MATTHEW: I believe that you are no more insane now than I believed you were before I read that.
LIZ: My favorite detail is the Vera Wang dress, which I also want.

Here's how I hoped it would go. Blades would read my fax and call me, and I'd say, "Oh, but how do I know it's really you?" and he'd say, "How can I prove it?" "Sing to me," I'd answer, because everyone has told me how gracious he is. Then I would have the exquisite pleasure of Ruben Blades serenading me over the telephone.

Here's how it really went. I waited a couple of weeks. No one got back to me. I faxed one more time, then waited another week. Then I called one more time. I never heard anything from anyone again.

NOſtALgiA

ABRIEF SUMMARY of my plans for what I'll do with the rest of my life:

Plan A. Sell Echo.

Plan B. Work in TV.

Plan C. Give Echo away.

Plan D. Hit the road and wander.

Plan E. Work at a gas station in the middle of nowhere, like Ellen Burstyn in the movie *Resurrection*.

Plan F. Take over as the new caretaker of Prospect Cemetery.

Plan G. Work at the Cat Practice cleaning cat cages.

I'm now adding Plan H: Apply for Jack Abrams's job when he retires. Jack Abrams is the founder and curator of a museum of all the schools in Huntington, Long Island, called the Heritage Room. He calls himself an "educational junk collector." Everyone in Huntington gives Jack whatever they find in their school basements and attics, as well as in their home basements and attics. Since 1986 he's been putting together an extensive collection of yearbooks, kindergarten chairs, science class displays, football uniforms, band uniforms, photographs, plaques, trophies, dioramas, slides, film strips, it's endless. He'll take anything. Jack Abrams is keeping the history of Huntington alive.

Abrams started the archive when he was fifty-five years old, after retiring as principal of the Jefferson School. The Nathan Hale School was about to close when he rescued fifteen boxes that contained, among other things, a collection of "excuse notes," some wrestling and math award plaques, and photographs of nineteen of the twenty graduates from the class of 1898, which currently hang on the back wall at the Heritage Room. (Among them is the photo of one Jesse F. Sammis, staring off into the distance.) The collection has since grown to fill three rooms at the Huntington Union Free School District Administration Building (formerly the Woodhull Elementary School). Jack's favorite artifacts are a Bible, a flag, *The Long Islander* (a local newspaper, which is still around), pens, inkwells, and several school notebooks that he found inside the 1923 cornerstone of a school that was torn down and whose name he has since forgotten.

When Jack was a boy he kept what he called secret chests, filled with his most precious objects. On rainy days he'd sit on the floor, savoring each one, going over their histories in his head. He would put together scrapbooks of photographs, newspaper articles and household artifacts, and his own neatly typed recollections and explanations: the world in his head transferred onto page after page of black construction paper.

I've been out to the Heritage Room twice. Both times I

searched for and found my junior high school yearbook. I wanted to look at the faces of all the people I'd lost touch with but never forgotten. The second time I went, Jack was giving a presentation about the collection to a large group of fourth-graders in a room that served as both the school cafeteria and auditorium. At one point he said, "Nobody likes to change," and at another, "I've been sad many times in my life because of changes." That's when I thought, *This is the job for me.* If I couldn't work in television or move my cats to the middle of nowhere, perhaps filling chests with the discarded treasures of Huntington children would be my best diminishing-the-power-of-death option. That, or tending graves.

pOLL

What do you miss the most from your youth?

This question inspired some of the most descriptive responses I'd ever read on Echo. And every one of them was sad.

I miss the garden in our house in Lebanon, which Syrian soldiers dug trenches in and ran over the flowers with their tanks and to this day won't let us visit. I used to play in that garden for hours, chasing lizards, but now there are just patches of dirt, dead grass, and big ugly tanks, and pornography which the soldiers put up all over the walls.

272

I miss the sense of an endless future. I miss the energy to do ten cartwheels. I miss my father, since if he had lived I would have been able to get to know him better.

The feeling that I can achieve anything I want to in the world.

I miss getting sick with excitement about birthdays and Christmas and not being able to sleep the night before.

The exhilaration of the last day of school.

Counting the days until something great, like Palisades Park.

I miss looking forward to being grown up. I always wondered what it would be like to have a job and live on my own, be married, and have kids. While some of these things still haven't happened, I've stopped feeling as if I would feel dramatically different after these events happen.

I miss Mom pulling down the shades, closing the closet doors, turning on the nightlight, and talking to my handpuppets as I hid under the covers.

Long summer evenings playing out back with my brothers and the neighborhood kids, and a game called Capture the Flag.

Getting carried from the car when I was sleepy.

Innocence.

Sixty-two percent said, essentially, "Feeling safe and free and taken care of." I'm one of the 62 percent. I miss lying on the grass, smelling the wisteria, listening to bobwhites—those days when all I had to decide was whether to go swimming or down to the corner to buy some Fruit Stripe gum.

Ten people said they didn't miss anything from their youth. "Not one minute."

cats

THE OTHER NIGHT Buddy sat in front of the stove for about twenty minutes. He just sat there, staring. It was as if he were channeling Veets, taking up the vigil for the mouse that ran underneath so many years before. Then, in a very Veets-like maneuver, he successfully knocked over fifty times his body weight in garbage. Twice. He was looking for more food. After that he played with Ping-Pong balls.

That's when I had to say good-bye to Veets. I don't want to do a Jimmy Stewart *Vertigo* thing with Buddy. He shouldn't have to sacrifice his tiny new life for a dead cat. So I wrote Veets's name on a piece of paper and burned it in the flame of my cinnamon-scented candle, and hoped once again that there is such a thing as life after death. *Thank you, Veets.*

It's okay, Buddy. You don't have to wait for that mouse. Go find yourself a new one. Or a bug. If you're hungry I'll feed you. If you

want to play I'll get you all the toys you want. Live your wonderful
new life. You're free.

Beamers has been sick ever since he sniffed Veets's death.
I've had to take him to the veterinarian on practically a weekly
basis. In three months I spent over a thousand dollars there.
Biologically he went haywire; I had to up the dosage on all his
medications. First it was a high fever. The next week it was
ringworm, then a cold so bad his face was perpetually wet from
his leaking eyes and nose and he wouldn't eat anything—not
Tender Vittles, not baby food, not the chicken or chicken livers
I cooked myself. Then the ringworm spread. It's been one
thing after the other. I understand, little Beams. Why can't
everything be the way it was? Just you and me and Veets on
the couch, happy to be together not doing much. It can't. Nothing lasts. Passages suck. I'll see you through this, babycat.

ruth Hunter

RUTH HUNTER WAS BORN on July 16, 1916, in Minneapolis and moved to California in 1944 with her six-year-old daughter, Sue Carol, a.k.a. Suki, when her then-husband got a medical discharge from the Army. Ruth has been widowed at least twice. Her first husband, the children's father, died when he was forty-nine, though they were already divorced by that time. Her marriage to husband number two lasted less than six months, and Ruth doesn't know or care about when or how he died. Her marriage to Carl—artist, musician, opera singer, music and math teacher, and the love of her life—lasted thirty years, until his death from melanoma. A very busy peace activist and writer, she has a master's degree in counseling and guidance, and at various times in her life has worked as an accountant, a teacher, and an adult school counselor. The miners and wholesalers she haggles with over deals on the materials she uses in her arts and crafts call her the Rock Lady.

Ruth Hunter looks twenty years younger than her age and seems completely at ease. When you ask her to talk about her life she talks about what she is doing now. She's more alive than I am, and she doesn't give the past a second thought—unless you insist.

Are you old?

Chronologically, it is an awesome yes. But I don't feel old.

When I was working on my master's, I spent six weeks in a senior nursing home. I still remember the sadness. Being old in a nursing home means only one way out—in a box. A lifetime of decision making has been reduced to trivia, and instead, powerlessness and hopelessness take over. The other day I visited a friend in a nursing home and felt sadness again. Old folks, sitting with blank stares, or heads nodding almost to their collarbone, alone and probably frightened.

That is exactly what it's like when I visit Lotte. Are they all like that?

On the other hand, being old with all faculties in place (sight, hearing, smell), it ain't bad. I can put up with a few creaky limbs. When I'm at the computer too long, or sitting on the grass at a picnic, I know it's harder to get up than when I was twenty, thirty, or forty. I'm okay as long as being old still means driving a car, going to a protest, getting arrested, making my own decisions, and living alone with my treasures and my dog Charlie Brown.

Which kind of old person will I be?

278

What are the main differences between the young you and you now?

I am wiser than I was at sixteen. . . .

When I was sixteen my home was rigid and intolerant: no dating, no makeup, and I wanted freedom. One day, with a train ticket and five dollars, I slipped away and rode to Chicago from Minneapolis. I had a friend I knew in the fourth grade and she said it would be all right if I came to live there and sleep on the couch. I was reading the job listings in the paper at a downtown coffee shop when a young man asked to join me. He suggested dinner and a movie but asked if I would mind going to his apartment first, where he would change. I did, and barely got out of a messy situation. Not very wise.

. . . and I'm more compassionate than I was in my thirties . . .

I was a mess. A two-year-old baby, a twelve-year-old, and a divorce in the wind. And school, full-time. I remember being overwhelmed. I still have twinges of guilt at my impatience with the children. One day, after a particularly frustrating early morning of braiding both of the girls' hair, I made an appointment and they both received haircuts, much to Suki's sadness and to my guilt that lingers. If I had been less harassed, I would have had more compassion for a near teenager and the need to be like her peers.

Did you have a midlife crisis? Was it a turning point? What effect did it have on the rest of your life?

Never. No age has ever been a crisis for me. Seems to me that mulling over age is a sheer waste of time. No matter how one frets, the inexorable passing of seconds, minutes, hours, and years will continue, so why waste energy.

I don't know. Does fretting help or make matters worse? It seems to be helping me.

How do you feel when you see your body in the mirror?

My body is really okay. Boobs a bit large, small waistline, great legs, and wrinkles well detailed. Not bad for a size 8.

What scares you?

Death in an abstract way, like it couldn't really happen to me. I really can't elaborate except to think about nothingness, and maybe regret no more blue skies and green hills and the tumbling waves I see almost every morning when Charlie and I walk.

Is there anything that no longer frightens you?

I am no longer frightened of cats.

Frightened of cats? Those amazing furballs of love?

Is there anything you no longer care about?

The more radical my lifestyle has become, the less I am trapped in the "buy me" mentality. There is a part of me that is stingy. I don't mind giving contributions to causes dear to me, but I have never been big on buying more than absolutely necessary, so even my refrigerator reflects my personal slightly anal lifestyle.

You are addressing someone you care about, someone young. Please finish this sentence: "If you only knew . . ."

. . . how exciting it is to take risks. Whenever I was getting ready for trips to Central America or Cuba, invariably I would get phone calls asking me if I knew what I was doing. But taking risks for altruistic reasons makes me feel so good. Once we were in Honduras. It was the heyday of death squads and disappearance and a group of maybe fifteen of us met with the Mothers of the Disappeared. While soldiers stood watching with guns visible, we joined the mothers who were holding large banners asking where their children were.

Perhaps it was risky, but the feeling of doing a decent thing gave me such great satisfaction, it was worth any risk. I'm glad I did it.

I need to get off the couch more.

Fast-forward to your deathbed. You're saying good-bye to friends and loved ones. Is there anything you've left unsaid that you'd like to say while you still have the chance?

Do what I did for my husband. I made a huge farewell party. Over a hundred people came and each brought one flower to bid him adieu. It would be fun if one of my kids did the same so I could say good-bye and then depart in dignity. I could use some music and a few jokes. I'm not big on tears. I hate the thought of a memorial, since I couldn't bear the schmaltzy things they would say. Half of them would probably be half-truths. What has been unsaid all these years between mothers and daughters had best be left unsaid when I die.

I can't imagine being so at peace I could get through my own good-bye party without having one long anxiety attack. But I'd like to think I might be someday. And that I'd have even ten friends who'd like to attend.

Which of your possessions would you hope will not be thrown out?

All of them.

What would you like to experience one last time?

Maybe male companionship; a little sex wouldn't hurt.

Looking back on it all, what will you miss the most? What are your most favorite things in the world? On a day-to-day basis, what are the things that give you pleasure?

281

Those almost-daily e-mails from Suki. Aside from my wonderful progeny, my daily delights would be a page or a chapter, my morning bridge game, and that hazelnut-flavored cup of French roast. And then, another favorite is taking Charlie out to smell the flowers after my daily shower, which means walking to the ocean. The other day I saw a white egret. Very exciting. After checking my e-mail, I like to make a protest call to a representative or president. There is always a crisis, whether East Timor, the World Trade conference, or finance reform. And then, maybe, that lovely glass of wine at the end of a busy day.

Whom will you miss the most?

A question moms would have a hard time to answer, especially me with two daughters, my two stepdaughters and stepdaughter-in-law, and grandkids. Must we always have a provocative either/or?

Was it worth it? Why?

What was my alternative? I hope life will continue for a while.

I couldn't visit Ruth. She lives in California, and unless I have to I don't like to be more than twelve hours away from my cats. I have a few pictures of her. I could see a bunch of big old graggly miners getting a kick out of her. She looks like she'd be up for anything. Ruth Hunter is game. I showed her daughter Suki what she said about her daily e-mail. Suki cried.

work

I'M SCREWED. Company B flaked out on me just the way every-one said they would. When I accepted their offer, all my friends said, "Do you have any idea who you're dealing with?" I did. Company B had a reputation. Their business until re-cently has been the processing and distribution of fats and oils, from a fish called menhaden, that are used in animal feed, in margarine, and as organic fertilizer. (Menhaden are also a source of the very healthy omega-3 fatty acids, but Company B hasn't gone to town on omega-3 yet.) Although they're still in the fish products business, Company B has decided that they want in on the Internet. They're not entirely clear what the Internet is or how they'll fit in, but they want to play. First they created a separate entity and made an all-stock offer to buy Excite, one of the largest companies on the Internet. Excite was valued at around $1.4 billion at the time, Company B at around $260 million. Excite wasn't interested. Because of "the vast disparity in the market capitalization of Excite and [Company B], and the complete lack of synergy between the two companies' businesses," they explained, the proposal, "would be vastly dilutive and holds no possible value to Excite's shareholders."

For a while Company B wanted to own Web sites. They did some research, took an ad out in *The New York Times* that said, "[Company B] will buy your Web site," then signed letters of intent to buy roughly thirty-one small Web sites, including Bianca Troll, producers of the famous *Bianca's Smut Shak.* They took it back a month later, issuing a statement that they would be returning to the marine-processing business. Lawsuits were filed. Two months after that, they announced they were back in: "We feel that the Internet continues to offer great opportunities for [Company B]." Four months after *that,* they took out another ad looking for Web sites, this time in *The Wall Street Journal.* And two months after that, they decided they wanted to try the virtual-community business and made their offer to me. The following spring, a nervous Company B employee who had just received a promotion called to tell me that they wouldn't be buying Echo after all. *Let the "I told you so"s begin.* Like the guy who makes promises, never commits, but still manages to get dates, Company B filled my head with sweet talk that made me forget all about the other "girls." I was smitten and it was going to be different with "us." *Well, sue,* I thought. Then I immediately envisioned this stern Judge Judy type looking at me and saying, "You knew their history. Are you trying to tell the court that it never occurred to you that you might be in for more of the same?" "But, but..." "Enough. The court declares you an idiot. Case closed."

After delaying completion of the sale for eight months— with very reasonable explanations and convincing promises of "Don't worry, it's a done deal, we're just busy" (they were preparing an IPO)—they did just what everyone said they'd do.

They changed their mind. In the meantime, I had had Echo on hold for eight months because Company B was in rule-the-world mode at the time and wanted Echo as is. When I tried to bill them for expenses associated with keeping Echo as is, they said, "We didn't know the problems the company has been having." "Did so." (I'd told them in writing and in e-mail and on the phone before they made me the offer. I even exaggerated the problems, and they made me the offer anyway.) "Did not." Then I reminded them of the memos I sent. "Submit an invoice," they told me. Then they didn't want to pay it. We agreed on a number so small I'm embarrassed to say what it was.

A week later they tried to get me to sign an agreement saying that the whole thing didn't, in fact, happen, and came up with a whole new version of events. They threw in a con-fidentiality clause that would have prevented me from telling any version. When I refused to sign off on their version and told them to take out the confidentiality clause, they tried to replace it with a nondisparagement clause. I logged into the Secret Space to tell my friends. Howard asked, "What's next? A non-rolling-your-eyes-when-Company B's-name-comes-up-at-parties clause?"

I refused the nondisparagement clause, and the same ner-vous, and now very flustered Company B employee said, "Well, then we're not going to pay you the money we agreed to." I offered to sign a clause stating that I would only tell the truth. "That way I can only tell what really happened and you can sue me if I don't." "We're not interested in the facts," he re-sponded. I gave him a chance to reword that, and he changed it to, "We're interested in the perception of the facts."

I made arrangements for another company to house all our equipment, then I got ready to close the office and work from home. Anyone who was still helping me out was doing so on-line, so I didn't need to keep the office. For weeks I almost

285

threw up every time I thought about how I had sat passively for eight months, believing I had a done deal. Everything was going to be okay. *Idiot.* Company B is still trying to make up its mind about what kind of Internet company it is going to be (and it never did pay me that teeny, tiny amount of money it said it would). And I'm on to Plans B through H.

beauty

HALFWAY THROUGH OUR FIRST SET at SOB's last week, I took off my glasses. I was sweating so much it was forming pools at the bottom of the rims and I couldn't see. "Do you really need to wear glasses?" a friend in my band asked. "You have such pretty eyes. Have you considered surgery?" I know she meant this in the nicest possible way. "Yes, I've considered surgery, but have you seen *A Clockwork Orange*?" I asked her. "Remember that scene where they force Malcolm McDowell's eyelids to remain open while they torture him? That's what they use when they operate on your eyes. And you're awake the whole time." I know my looks are fading, but I'm not willing to do what it takes to look better. My friend's question only reminded me that I am walking around not looking as good as I could.

I resent having options that I don't want to take. I never

did get the liposuction for my stomach. The bulge went away when Veets died. A slight change in my diet and it was gone. I also never sprang for the veneers for my teeth. I found out I could tinker with a few less radical things and look basically okay. So I haven't moved beyond my beauty issues, I've only temporarily gotten *around* them.

I read a Steve Martin interview in which he talks about what he calls his "last viable decade." According to Martin, this refers to the last decade when you still look relatively okay and can continue to attract at least some people. I'm in my last viable decade, I've decided. A survey in *People* magazine indicated that most women consider age fifty-four to be "the end of youth," so it looks like I've got my timing right. This is it. I'm down to the wire. What am I willing to do about it? Not much.

I'm hoping I look good enough. I've always been told I look much younger than my actual age, but I don't know. I went to a party with a bunch of people my age a few months ago. I was talking about the history of Echo and what I wanted to do with it now. They all gave me advice, but not as peers, but in this older-and-wiser way. And they were asking me questions that suggested they were trying to get "the young person's point of view." Finally I asked them how old they thought I was. Twentysomething, they said. I'm forty-three as I write this.

The thing is, if you put me next to someone who actually *is* in her twenties, I would stop looking like someone in her twenties. I'm convinced of this. It's not that I look in my twenties, it's something about how I act—some trick of the eyes—that makes me seem younger. Maybe the people at that party wanted to believe my face was that of a woman in her twenties, because if they thought they looked older than me it would mean that they must look in their fifties or sixties.

A woman named Evelyn recently posted on Echo that all her friends say she looks as if she's in her twenties. I know

Evelyn. She doesn't look as if she's in her twenties. I'd say she looks my age or older. My first thought was, If someone (and her friends) could be that wrong about her appearance, I might be equally wrong about my own. But it didn't make me think that the people who say I look so young are right. What I thought was, *Maybe my last viable decade is already, irrevocably over.*

deAtH

I TOOK ONE LAST SHOT at learning the identity of my ghost. I have another neighbor who has lived in my building since the fifties—Mary Lou. I didn't approach her sooner because, frankly, I'm a little afraid of her. Sometimes she looks at me funny. She was perfectly friendly, however, when she told me that Lotte was confused when she said there was a man who abused his wife on one floor, and a different man who died and wasn't found for weeks on another. Those men were one and the same, Mary Lou told me. And this man had lived, was cruel to his wife, and died, undiscovered, in *my* apartment. All the flies that flew into Lotte's apartment years ago? Came from my place. "Something bad happened in there," Mikal had said. A lot of bad things, apparently. "I think her name was Min," Mary Lou said. "She was a small woman. And she married late in life." Up until her marriage, Min lived one block away with her parents. Once she got married, her parents never came to her new home to see her. When Lotte told me about a woman who wandered the halls when she was afraid to go into her apartment, she was talking about Min.

One night, in the middle of a hot summer, when Min was dying, she leaned over the railing—my railing—and started calling out, "I'm cold. It's so cold." She sounded so pitiful. She wouldn't let up. "I'm so cold," she kept crying. Finally, even though it was sweltering, the super sent up some heat. No one in the building complained. She was dying. Min and her husband lived in my apartment from the fifties through the late seventies and they never had any children or pets.

Mary Lou told me to double-check her information with Salvador. Salvador has lived in my building since the sixties. I telephoned him. "Mary Lou is the one who's mistaken. Your apartment was empty for thirty years," he said. From sometime in the fifties—the time my ghost lived there, according to Mikal—to the early eighties, my apartment was vacant. In Salvador's version, after whatever happened happened, and it must have been bad, no one lived there for another three decades.

I looked up at the place where Mikal said my ghost hovers. "Are you Min?" I asked, then immediately said, "Oh, please, don't answer that!" I'm not ready to see or hear her yet. But I'd like to work up the nerve.

faNtaſy

EMMA STEWART, the former caretaker of Prospect Cemetery, isn't buried in Prospect Cemetery. She's buried in Evergreen Cemetery in Brooklyn. I literally made myself seasick whipping through the microfilm reader looking for her. I didn't know the exact date of her death—all I knew was that it was spring 1954—so I had to scan every day of every Long Island newspaper to find it. I was afraid to go the bathroom to throw up because some guy was waiting to use my machine. He looked like the kind of person who would have moved my things while I was gone and taken over. *She couldn't have died in March, could she?* I thought, every time I had to stop because of the nausea. No. She died on May 9, ten days before her fifty-third birthday. The death notice I found didn't indicate how she had died or where; it only said she was buried in

Evergreen Cemetery and that she was survived by her two sons, Richard and Owen.

Her plot is in such a sorry, dusty little spot. There's almost no grass, only dirt and stones and one tree. To get to Evergreen Cemetery one Friday afternoon I walked through the East New York section of Brooklyn. What a weird, time-forgotten place it was. I felt as if I had been transported to a bad part of town out of the 1950s; everyone's clothes were early Marlon Brando–Levi's; there were lots of five-and-dimes, an industrial racket, and dripping from the L and A trains overhead. Relatively normal-looking people were mixed in with disturbing urban-Appalachian-*Deliverance* types, and some pretty mean-looking people were walking slowly past other people doing their best to at least look pretty mean. It was a depressed and seedy David Lynch sort of neighborhood, and once again I thought, *I could live here.* The people were mostly friendly. When I got off the bus, the driver escorted me to the block that led to Evergreen.

At the cemetery a caretaker gave me a ride to Siloam, the section where Emma Stewart lies. "It's a long walk," he told me. "Siloam" is from the Bible, the name of a river where the blind are made to see. The caretaker and I rode past pleasant sections with huge, lovely stones and statues to a section with only patches of grass and the occasional knocked-over marker.

There I found Emma's lonely and bare spot, so different from the graves in Prospect Cemetery. While Evergreen is clearly active and tended, and Prospect almost completely forgotten, Prospect is green and wild and fragrant. Evergreen is cold and dead-feeling. Emma was buried with a child named Robert, who died when he was five. I'm guessing he was her son. No one else was mentioned on her stone with her, not her husband and, thankfully, not her other two sons, who would be sixty-seven and seventy-five if still alive.

There wasn't much to see, but I stayed for a while, imagining a conversation with Emma and a few others from my dead-people support system: my grandmother Daisy, my great-great-grandmother Ellen, the ghost from my apartment, and Sonya from *War and Peace*. Sonya isn't even real, but then how real are these dead women I'd never met when they *were* real?

Emma stands behind her headstone and watches me without expression.

ME: Why did you end up here, Emma?
EMMA: I couldn't tell you.
ME: Well, what does it matter? You're dead. I'll be dead. Everyone who knows you will be dead.

She looks pained for a moment, then smiles politely.

EMMA: They're all here. The Sammises, the Baylises, and everyone else under all those graves and all the myrtle, mugwort, and ivy.

I see endless, indistinct crowds of dead people behind her, everyone who has ever lived, murmuring softly, making a collective sound like a million TVs coming through the walls from another room.

ME: What am I going to do?
DAISY: What are your choices?
ME: Oh, Grandma. You were so gypped, Grandma. Can I call you Grandma?
DAISY: Of course.
ELLEN: I'm Great-Great-Grandma!
SONYA: I was an aunt. Sorta.

We all turn to look at my ghost, who hasn't said anything yet.

GHOST: It's nice to get out of your apartment.
ME: Yes. Well. It's hard to believe it's all going to end.
I'm not at the beginning of my life, wondering what's
going to happen. It *is* happening.
DAISY: Make it count.
ME: And how do I do that?
DAISY: Don't look at me. I was locked up and halluci-
nating at the end.
ELLEN: I think I may have been drinking. (Rosemary,
my second cousin once removed, says there was talk that
Ellen drank.)
GHOST: I was hiding out.
ME: Sistah! (We high-five.)
SONYA: I'm not real.
ME: Sorry.

*We stand in a semicircle around Emma's grave and stare down.
Emma looks frightened.*

EMMA: I thought there was something else in store for
me. I never thought that digging graves would be the last
thing I ever did.
ME: I hope you were happy.

*She doesn't answer. No one says anything for a minute. We squint
our eyes and look into the seemingly infinite dead and try to distinguish
one person from another.*

ME: So this is it. Time is moving really fast now. I'll be
dead soon.
EMMA: That's about the size of it.

295

ME: Not a big size, is it?

DAISY: What are you complaining about? Look at my life.

ME: I know it's pathetic for me to be sitting here and the worst thing I have to worry about is that I am going to die someday. Boo-hoo. Get a life. I know.

I look at Sonya. She was in somewhat the same position. I'm hoping she'll be on my side.

SONYA: Don't look at me, I'm fictional.

ME: Did Tolstoy have a happy end? I wonder. Because I don't see how he could. All his characters end up with such lifeless twilight years. Even the ones who had supposedly happy endings.

DAISY: Look who's talking.

ME: Yeah. Me and Leo. Two of a kind.

I look at her.

ME: You know, would it kill you to act a bit more grandmotherly?

Daisy looks at Ellen, her grandmother, for help.

ELLEN: Oh? Do you think I have any answers?

ME: No one has any answers. I don't have any answers. What answer could there possibly be? We have to die.

EMMA: Er . . .

DAISY: Um . . .

We all turn to Sonya, who looks defensive.

SONYA: Still fictional!

EMMA: What do you want, Stacy?

ME: I don't know. I have a few plans. But how do I know which is the right plan?

DAISY: You're not insane, are you?

ELLEN: Or drunk?

SONYA: And you're real.

ME: Well, there's that.

GHOST: And maybe you can come back.

They look as if they want to say more, as if they're racking their brains trying to come up with something useful. They're angry, frustrated, and sad, but they try. I prepare to act pleased with whatever they say. I don't want to make them feel any more helpless than they feel already.

SONYA: I hope you figure it out.

GHOST: I've been watching you for years. I think you're making progress.

DAISY: We're rooting for you. We're on your side, all of us.

ELLEN: I'm glad you found us. It's nice to be remembered again.

EMMA: You know, I *was* happy digging those graves.

I really think that's what Emma would say, even though that is also what I'd like her to say. Because maybe someday that will be me.

poLL

FROM A POLL OF 110 PEOPLE ON ECHO:

You've got the rest of your life in front of you. What do you look forward to?

Twenty-one percent said, "I look forward to love."
Nineteen percent said having children or watching their children grow up.
Ten percent said owning a home.
Ten percent said travel.
Ten percent said being free from debt or having more money.
Ten percent said retirement.

A number of people were looking forward to food. One wrote, "The next episode of *The Sopranos*." Another wrote, "Everything except death." And a good friend of mine wrote, "Nothing. Stacy, your damned questions upset me."

Put me with the people who look forward to love. What else is there to look forward to, really, when you don't have love? I don't want to die without love. Someone like me is going to read my book someday and wonder, "Did she ever find it?" And maybe someone will know and say, "Nope. I heard she died alone with a bunch of cats." And the someone like me will reply, "That's so sad." Then, if she's really like me, she will wonder, *Could that happen to me?*

tHe eNd

AND YET I'M HAPPY. My midlife crisis is over. I don't have an anxiety attack just because I believe the following contradiction is true: life is hard, nothing lasts, then you die; and it's not all that bad really, and you never know, it could get better. Is this an elaborately constructed state of denial? Maybe an elaborately constructed state of denial is the best response, the only response.

I'm still not in a serious relationship. "What am I supposed to do without the man of my dreams?" I asked my friend Chris, and she replied, "When there's no romance in your life, have a romance with life." If you can't have one true love, fall in love with everyone and everything a little. Which is what I do now. I take love wherever I can, in smaller bits and pieces, from the Secret Space, and my drumming friends, from everyone I know, and my lovely little cats. Sometimes it adds up, sometimes it doesn't. The important point is, it works enough.

I don't look as good as I used to, it's true, and soon I won't look good at all. I heard Ellen Foley sing a few months ago. Ellen Foley is another ex-girlfriend of my friend Aly, who dated Maria, the Italian woman who isn't aging well. Ellen, Maria, and I are all roughly the same age. My last image of Ellen is from 1977. She's sitting on Aly's lap while we zip around Manhattan, going to parties with people from all over the world who are all going places. It was so exciting. People like Ellen were so exciting. She was a singer. She had just recorded the song "Paradise by the Dashboard Light" on a Meatloaf album.

I saw Ellen for the first time in over two decades at the Losers Lounge. At a club not far from where I live, every few months a guy named Joe McGinty puts on a musical show that he calls the Losers Lounge. First he picks a songwriter or band, such as Burt Bacharach, Dusty Springfield, or the Zombies. Then he gets twenty or more performers to get up one after another and do a version of their songs. I love the music, the singers, the club, Joe, and especially the audience, which screams and claps for every singer, whether they're good or not. Sometimes people dance on the tables, acting like this is the best possible place to be. I love getting caught up in that. You can always count on the Losers Lounge to provide a moment of glory.

Ellen Foley came to the Losers Lounge and belted out a rendition of the Abba song "The Winner Takes It All," and she had the audience beside themselves, screaming and pounding on the tables and the floor. When I'd run into Maria, all I could think about was the things in my life that were over. Ellen, on the other hand, made me think about what's still left. When you look at Ellen's face, you don't see a dead-and-gone girl. She has aged every bit as much as Maria, but she doesn't look haunted.

I don't feel haunted. Not long after Veets died Mauro took me to a concert of the seventeenth-century British composer John Dowland. All his songs are about death—I was so glad to have gone. There are moments in life when the last thing in the world you want to do is be cheered up. You need to wallow. This was written in the program notes: "Meditating on a beautiful expression of sadness can help to provide a thoroughly uplifting sense of consolation." I have wallowed and panicked my way through my midlife crisis and I had one last wallowing thing to do. Last night I sang Brahms's *Requiem* with the Grace Church Choral Society. This piece is a sublimely beautiful expression of sadness and in my mind I dedicated our performance to Veets. I put all the grief I had into it. My greatest pleasure and my greatest release turned out to come from watching John, our conductor. There were moments during the performance when he half closed his eyes, leaned back, and, with something like a smile, turned his head from side to side—as if he were both with us and on the very edge of heaven. His face expressed rapture, and I loved being part of the music that transported him there. I was lifted out of myself and my small moment and my small life and put along the eternal conveyer belt of humanity doing what it can to transform sorrow and fear. "Blessed are they that mourn," the *Requiem* begins, "for they shall be comforted." I mourned my youth and I feel comforted. "They that go forth and weep and carry precious seed, shall return with joy," it continues. It ends with "Blessed are the dead which die in the Lord from now on. 'Yes,' says the spirit, 'that they rest from their labors, and that their works follow after them.' " Okay, the Lord part, ew, but the second line, "their works follow," I'm okay with that.

My midlife crisis ended, I think, because I finally let go of the life preserver I had been holding on to my whole life. My arms were tired. *If I'm going to drown, I'd just as soon drown already, rather than live in fear of drowning for the rest of my life.*

I don't care about success the way I used to. I don't even care about actually getting what I want. I just want possibility. The sheer joy of possibilities, that things can still happen, that's the most exciting part. Whether they do or not is not important.

What's important is that it's not over. *Meine seele verlanget und sehnet:* My soul longs and sighs. Another line from Brahms's *Requiem*. I've changed my mind. I want to long and sigh as long as I live.

I don't want to appear too optimistic and uplifting. Good things may still happen, but it really is all downhill from here, and then we have to die. There's simply no out. "Somewhere over the rainbow, skies are blue . . ." Then a rock falls on your head and kills you.

Some of my friends comfort themselves with sentiments such as "We're made up of energy and energy doesn't die." I don't care if I continue as pure energy. I want *me*—my personality and my memories—to continue. Otherwise, what good does it do *me*?

In a moment of panic and dread about being alone forever, someone turned to my friend Howard for reassurance. She wanted someone to tell her that she wouldn't die alone. "Well," he told her, "in an existential sense, of course you'll die alone. We all do. But in the other sense, I'm sure you'll die with a loved one holding your hand.

"Afterward, of course, he'll say, 'Ew! Cadaver hand!' but you won't hear him."

What do we learn as we grow old? We learn how to be forty or fifty or sixty or seventy or eighty.

Rick Carrier said, "You are in charge of what you are, have been, and will be, and if you do not accept this you will become everything you do not want to become." I no longer know what I don't want to become. It used to be "a woman living alone with cats," but that's what I'm doing now and I'm happy.

Mikal visited my apartment to give me a ghost update. He told me that everything had changed. Instead of hovering in one corner over the couch, my ghost was moving around. It felt better. "You've done something that has soothed the ghost *a lot*! I'm trying to figure out exactly what, because it is so much more at peace." Maybe it's because I'm somewhat at peace.

Last night I played in a new band called Mulher da Samba, and twice I completely fucked up. Normally that would have ruined my evening. Instead, I simply apologized for messing up. "I don't know what happened, I completely spazzed out." I was so relaxed. Did learning how to drum get me to the point where I no longer care that I am not the greatest drummer in the world, and that I will never be a rock star? Or was it clearing away the weeds on the grave of someone who also never became a rock star? Or was it looking up all those born the same day I was, then buried on Hart Island a couple of weeks later?

I don't know. Admitting things, I think, is the key. The important thing is that I can admit everything I want and feel, even if it makes me look odd and pathetic. I can pretend I'm not the way I am, and be miserable, or I can admit that I love clearing away weeds, and finding Emma's tomb, and giving Beamers his drip every other day, and be happy. It makes me feel good to admit I like finding the remaining traces of people who are dead and gone. I admit I was glad to be able to ease the passing of a creature with whom I never exchanged a single word.

It adds up to a life. All the things I did to long and sigh and wallow finally amounted to something. They don't make death acceptable, but they make living more acceptable. I realize this could be yet more evidence that I'm winding down. The biological drugs have kicked in and I'm being drugged into indifference. I no longer care if I can't tell the difference between denial and acceptance and giving up, or whether I am admitting or surrendering to the natural process of growing older and slower.

I do realize that I'm incredibly lucky, all things considered. I have my health—blah, blah, blah—but knowing that doesn't help when you're in the thick of things. I also know I still have and will always have my problems. When they say that happiness is internal, I don't think they mean being so perfectly happy in the dreams inside your head. I have to make sure I don't bury myself there.

What makes dying okay? Nothing. No amount of accomplishment or love. I've given this a lot of thought. An elaborately constructed state of denial is the only way.

I find answers to life's questions on television. George Clooney said on TV, "I don't believe in happy endings but I believe in happy travels because I believe that ultimately, the ending is that you have a couple of options. The couple of options are: you die at a very young age, or you live long enough to watch your friends die. It's a mean life." He's right. There are no happy endings, unless you think dying can be a happy thing—in which case you're in for a nasty shock, according to Sherwin B. Nuland. My advice: stay active, have as good a time as you can, and do something to help someone else do the same. I believe we have a few more options than George believes, but he's right: it's a mean life.

And so short. More TV wisdom. I was watching Roberto Benigni on Joan Rivers's Oscar pre-show. She asked him, "How was your year?" "It was not a year," he answered. "It went by like a second." He rephrased her question: "How was your second?"

I don't think there are any great revelations out there. Nothing that can be summed up in a few words, at least. No one knows what it all means. And if our lives don't mean anything—if they are what they are and this is all there is—then "this" becomes even more important. Cormac McCarthy has a character who reviles "the true horror of death, the impersonal relentlessness of time," and "the absence of God from the world." I'm with him on death and time, but given the true horror of death and impersonal relentlessness of time, the absense of God makes life matter more.

I find it comforting—and liberating—to admit that I don't know anything. Neither does anyone else. And there's no Great Withholding Being up above who does either. I'm like Alistair Sim in *A Christmas Carol*, dancing for joy when he wakes up and realizes that the spirits have opened his eyes all in one night and it's Christmas! He still has his present. And the chance to alter his future. He sings, in that childish singsong way, "I don't know anything, I never did know anything, but now I know that I don't know, all in a Christmas morning. I must stand on my head."

I don't know anything.

I don't know what electricity is.

I don't know how a bill becomes law.

I don't know when life begins.

I don't know if God exists.

I don't know how to keep the weeds from growing over the graves at Prospect Cemetery.

I don't know how to ease Lotte's suffering.

I don't know if I'm going to find the man of my dreams.

I don't know how to keep my cats alive.

I don't know.

But now I know that I don't know. I must stand on my head. I'm still alive. And I can alter my future. Not that I will, of course, but there's the possibility, and that's something.

I did learn one thing. I found out that if you fall onto the subway tracks and don't have time to get back on the platform before the train comes, it's best to look for the "clear-up space." The clear-up space is the hole cut out of the wall; it's sometimes outlined in white. If you can't find a clear-up space, stand between the pillars on the other side of the track—your body facing the tracks, your head turned to the side—and hold on. Your last option: lie down in the center of the tracks.

I also found out that at present there are six Sammises in the Huntington school system. They'll be graduating from Huntington High School someday. When I found them I felt like I had hit the death-diminishing jackpot. Again, admitting things is key, so I don't want to pretend that I have reached some blissful state of enlightenment. My first thought was *Fine*.

I hope they all grow up to create nasty billing problems for all the rest of you who will live on after I die. But it does makes me feel better to know that there might always be Sammises joining that eternal conveyer belt of humanity, doing what they can to transform sorrow and fear. I'm one in a long line. I'm not alone. I never was and I never will be. If I find glory out of moments like these, I can live with that. I'll be right here waiting—with my friends and my cats, in between panic and joy, youth and old age and death, living from one moment of glory to the next and hoping that Tolstoy was right. I won't feel the bad things so keenly.

acknowledgments

Jack Abrams, from the Heritage Room, Long Island.

Jerry Allen, Calvary Cemetery.

Harry Bahrenburg, from the Huntington Crescent Club, Long Island.

Tim Bent, my editor. (Special thank you to Tim for being such a great editor and for being *my* editor.)

Jacqueline Broner, friend.

Michelle Brown, from Cypress Hills National Cemetery, Brooklyn, New York.

Red Burns, friend.

Rick Carrier, from the USA Bald Eagle Command, New York.

Marcelle Clements, friend.

Velma Dove, Pilgrim Psychiatric Center.

Lotte Faderwick, my former neighbor.

Dr. Janet Ficarra at the Downtown Veterinary Clinic.

Mikal Gilmore, friend and ghost-adviser.

Mary Lou Hofsoos, neighbor.

Melinda Hunt, author of *Hart Island*.

Ruth Hunter, one of my interviewees and my friend Sue Leonard's mother.

Josh Karpf, friend and suggestion-maker.

Richard Kasparian, from the Marble Cemetery, New York.

Valerie Katane, from the Oakwood Cemetery, Long Island.

Anna Kinnison, from the Daughters of the Union Veterans on the Civil War.

Maria A. Klesin, St. John's Cemetery.

Betsy Lerner, my agent. (Special thank you to Betsy for using all your talents on my behalf and for being a dark-side soulmate.)

Cate Ludlam from Prospect Cemetery, Jamaica, New York.

Tom McCarthy, from the New York City Department of Corrections.

Rosemary McCoy, my second-cousin once removed.

Howard Mittlemark, friend and suggestion-maker.

William Moloney, from Cypress Hills Cemetery, Brooklyn, New York.

Dimos Panagoulias, from the Shore Hotel, Coney Island.

Julia Pastore, editorial support from the younger generation.

Shirley Perry, from the Daughters of the Union Veterans on the Civil War.

Marianne Petit, friend.

Salvador Pimentel, neighbor.

Beatrice Richter, one of my interviewees and my friend Elizabeth Zimmer's mother.

Joe Rosen, friend and pain-in-the-ass.

Susanne Rosen, one of my interviewees and my friend Joe Rosen's mother.

Capt. Eugene Rupport, from the New York City Department of Corrections.

Anthony Scotti, from the Bay Shore Funeral Home, Long Island.

Richard Snow, author of *Coney Island: A Postcard Journey to the City of Fire*.

Sally Spooner, from City Critters, New York.

Dr. Sullivan and Doctor Shimel and everyone at the Cat Practice. (Special thank you to the Cat Practice for taking such good care of Veets and Beams and Buddy.)

John Tangora, from the Huntington Crescent Club, Long Island.

Katherine Twomey, age eight, the artist who did my cover.

Gail Vachon, friend.

Jeffrey Zaleski, my former husband. (Special thank you to Jeff for being my friend all these years.)